Daily Spiritual Renewal:

Help for Your Journey

Beverly Coker, Ph.D.

Printed in the United States of America

First Printing, 2019

Imprint: Independently published

The Writery Ink, LLC
Bloomfield, CT

ISBN: 9781677867332

Cover design: Rev. Sophia Walters

Disclaimer: The author (Beverly Coker, Ph.D.) and her assigns, do not accept any liability for intentional or unintentional plagiarism. The contributors to the Devotional *Daily Spiritual Renewal: Help for Your Journey* bear responsibility for the content of their work and retain all rights to their own contribution.

DEDICATION

To the late Vincent and Nerissa Sewell (my parents) who laid the foundation, and to my family and friends who impacted my life.
To each of you I say,
THANK YOU

CONTENTS

ACKNOWLEDGMENTS

This book would not be possible without the support of my husband, Tom Coker, who has always been my chief cheerleader. Special thanks to my children Lemu and Nerissa, whose love for me is unconditional.

To my sisters and brothers who have traveled this journey of life with me and have been my unwavering rock.

I would like to thank my many friends who have supported my idea to write this devotional. In particular, I want to thank my friend Monica Case Williams, who has worked diligently with me to bring the idea of this book to fruition Monica is a childhood friend with whom I had lost contact until the Lord reconnected us, just in time for her to be my sounding board on this journey.

I wholeheartedly also want to thank those who made contributions to this Devotional. You answered the call and so generously shared your wisdom, experience, and relationship with God with our readers. Your submissions are the most important component of this book. Undoubtedly, I could not have completed this assignment by myself, so with that I say, "Thank you."

I would like to recognize my prayer partner Carmen Burke who prayed me through many situations. To my church family whose love and support have propelled me forward, thank you for believing in me.

To the readers of this Devotional, I wish to thank you for your commitment to reading this book. It is my hope that your life will be spiritually enriched.

Finally, and most of all, thanks be to God, because without Him, this book would not be possible.

FOREWORD

We are living in a time that has been experiencing dramatic cultural shifts concerning spiritual values and the knowledge of God; however, God does not change, neither does his word *Malachi 3 verse 16*. It is, therefore, very timely that Dr. Beverly Coker was moved and inspired by the Holy Spirit to compile this Devotional at such a pivotal time.

This Devotional is written with passion and fervor, encouraging the believer to have daily intimate encounters with God in prayer and the reading of the Word of God. Many of the Devotionals speak directly to areas of our lives that need divine healing from an Omnipotent but personal God. Today, people find themselves in a state of hopelessness and despair. In this book, they will find **strength**, **guidance**, **direction**, and **faith** to believe God for the miraculous and the supernatural. Every page of this Devotional points to a loving Savior who cares about our every need and who is willing and ready to hear and answer our prayers. As you read this Devotional, a desire in you will be ignited to seek the presence and power of an Almighty God who can move the mountains that seem to overwhelm you and to deepen your spiritual walk.

Bishop Dr. Jonathan Ramsey, Jr.

Senior Pastor, Rehoboth Church of God, Bloomfield, Connecticut

THE CALL TO WRITE THIS DEVOTIONAL

"Take now thy son, thine only son, Isaac, whom thou lovest, and get the unto the land of Moriah and offer him there for a burnt offering upon one of the mountains which I will tell thee of."

--Genesis 22: 2

"By faith, Abraham, when he was called to go out into a place which he should after receive for an inheritance, obeyed; and he went out not knowing whither he went."

-- Hebrews 11: 8

I was in a private time of worship one morning when the voice of God spoke to me and placed in my spirit the idea of writing a Devotional. My first inclination was to doubt the authenticity of the voice and to doubt my ability to take on such a task; however, the call for this assignment did not diminish with time, with much rest, nor with reasonable excuses. The urge became more intense as I sought God's guidance. To validate the call, I consulted with other believers who enthusiastically endorsed the project and agreed to become contributors. I was encouraged by their responses. I invited them to share their experiences and wisdom garnered on their journey of life. Many confessed that they also entertained similar interests to write but had never mustered the courage to begin.

As I pondered the possibility of writing this Devotional, I became aware of the personal benefits of delving more deeply into the Word of God. Indeed, in addition to myself, there are people who want to grow spiritually, and this might be a means of helping to satisfy their hunger for God on a daily basis.

Today, you begin a journey with me. I recall Abraham leaving the safety and comfort of his Homeland for a country that was unknown. he embarked on his journey with Faith in a God who had already made and kept promises to him. Like Abraham, you and I will travel this journey together to daily experience God in His sovereignty, abundance, and everlasting love. As we begin this exciting quest to discover more of God's treasures, my prayer is that you will develop a deeper awareness of God's presence, peace, and revelation.

There will be days when the road gets bumpy, the terrain unfamiliar, and you are left to wonder why; however, like Abraham who exercised faith in God who had proven to Abraham to be a promise keeper, you and I will find that His promises to us are as relevant today as they were to Abraham and to countless others including Joshua "will not fail thee, nor forsake thee." (Joshua 1: 15).

Let us go forward in faith, with our eyes fixed on the One who is unchangeable, unable to fail, and always with us. it is my prayer that this Devotional will enrich and nurture your spiritual life.

Prayer

Father, we look to you in faith as we embark on a journey that is unknown to us but known to You. We ask You to be our guide and our light through all circumstances of our lives. We give You praise!

Beverly Coker

PURPOSEFUL LIVING

Be Nourished

"Blessed are they who hunger and thirst after righteousness for they shall be filled."

--Matthew 5:6

Hunger and thirst can be devastating and all-consuming to the extent that one cannot focus on anything else. Prolonged periods without food can cause pain, discomfort, weakness, and other physical illnesses. It is futile having a conversation with someone who is hungry or thirsty because they cannot focus on anything but satisfying the need for food or water.

Hungering and thirsting after righteousness can be painful but come with the promise that those desires will be satisfied. There should be a constant desire to draw close to God and seek after his righteousness through prayer, reading the word, and praise and worship. This is what makes us healthy, strong, and able to resist the fiery darts of the devil.

As we need physical food to sustain our bodies, so do we need spiritual food to sustain our souls. We often take care of our physical needs when we are physically malnourished and dehydrated. Spiritual snacks cannot satisfy; what is needed is a balanced spiritual meal. This is met by praying, reading the Word, and spending quality time seeking God.

"THOSE WHO DWELL IN THE SECRET PLACE OF THE MOST HIGH SHALL ABIDE UNDER THE SHADOW OF THE ALMIGHTY."

-- Psalm 91:1

It takes the disciplines of prayer, fasting and the study of the Word in order for spiritual hunger to be satisfied. It is no accident that you are reading this article today. God is extending the opportunity to you to be spiritually fed. Come and drink because He is water and eat, because He is food. Come to the table on which is spread a bountiful supply. There is room at the table for you.

"On the last greatest day of the festival, Jesus stood and said in a loud voice, 'Let anyone who is thirsty come to me and drink. Whoever believes in me as the scripture has said, rivers of water will flow from within them."

--John 7: 37 -38 (*NIV*).

Prayer

Lord, please help me to spend quality time with you so that I will be able to maintain a constant hungering and thirsting after righteousness and be satisfied. Amen!

Joy Wilson

Spirituality in the Workplace

"Let your light shine…they may see your good deeds, moral excellence and glorify our Father."

--Matthew 5:16

The workplace is a fertile environment for discipleship and ministry where there are many unsaved, hurting, hopeless people; however, your job is your priority and you should guard against freely witnessing in the workplace as this could be problematic

So, what are some effective ways to minister? God's solution is, "Let your light shine." Light illuminates darkness. It shows the way; it attracts and changes the atmosphere. How then to shine?

1. *Ask God to give you territory*. He will divinely connect you with those in need. Pray over your environment daily and remain alert in the spirit.
2. *Ask God for strategies*. Become the solution, not the problem. Cultivate friendships which can lead to opportunities for sharing as you become established as an ambassador for Christ.
3. *Ask God for wisdom*. You'll know what and went to speak. He has given us the tongue of the learned (see Isaiah 50: 4). Speak well of others. Avoid negative conversations.

When feasible, share gems from your trophy room about God's love and blessings in your life, your family, and friends. Create a thirst through *moral excellence* by His Spirit. Your light will break forth, and amazingly, you'll become the go to person when colleagues are faced with needs or crises.

There is truth in the saying, "What you are speaks so loudly, I cannot hear what you say." Live intentionally so your light illuminates the workplace to the glory of God.

Prayer

Father, thank you for the privilege to represent you. May I always be a light to show others the way and your Love, in Jesus' Name. Amen.

Monica Case Williams

Total Surrender to God

"I am crucified with Christ; nevertheless, I live. Yet not I, but Christ lives in me."

-- Galatians 2: 20

Some years ago, there was a popular gospel song which was basically a testimony of the writer who had a miraculous escape from a dangerous accident. With her infant strapped in the back seat of her car, she was hurrying to her destination and traveling too fast. On approaching a sudden turn in the road, she realized she was in danger. "Jesus, take the wheel," she shouted, and seconds later, she overturned and skidded to rest on the opposite side of the road.

Her child was unscathed and she herself was okay except for the fright. She had no recollection of what happened after she shouted, "Jesus, take the wheel." We often ask for God to be by our side or with us in times of various difficult situations. Because He is God and full of grace and mercy, He hears our cry and His will prevails; however, from this passage of scripture, Paul encourages us to be even more committed and surrender to Him at all times (Galatians 2: 20). We should literally live our lives every day as if we no longer live but it is Christ who lives in us.

Yes, we know miracles and supernatural events occur when Jesus takes the wheel as a songwriter experienced. After all, He is God and hears, sees, and knows it all and can do the impossible; therefore, we should allow Him to be the driver at all times.

There is a lot we can do to overcome pride, ego, and our own desires for self-gratification, but we must surrender. Ask for His help through prayers.

Prayer

Father, I surrender all. All to thee I owe. Amen.

JAT

God Has Not Forgotten You

"For I know the thoughts that I think toward you, saith the Lord. Thoughts of peace and not of evil to give you an expected end."

-- Jeremiah 29: 11

We have been created in the image of God and we are loved by Him. Sometimes, life gets rough and the first thing the enemy tries to scare us with is the thought of God forgetting about us; however, we know that God will never forget His children. God has great thoughts for us. His thought is to give us peace in His Shalom; this peace allows us to ride the waves of life. Although we may go through the Valley of the Shadow of Death, we can still rely on His peace because His peace is forever.

Just imagine, the Almighty God has good thoughts for us in our good times and in our bad times. In moments when we are discouraged or frustrated, His thought is still the same. He promises thoughts of peace and an unexpected end instead of evil. Today, let us not allow any other voice to silence the voice of God. Instead, rest assured that He will bring to pass that which He has said. Isaiah 55: 8 & 11 reminds us that God's thoughts are not our thoughts, and God's ways are not our ways, and that His words will never return to Him without being fulfilled.

Prayer

Eternal Father, I come to you with praise and thanksgiving for your fatherly love for us. Every day is new in your great love. With your love, we can live victoriously depending not in ourselves, but in your great and mighty love. Every day you give us your peace and we are grateful. Thank you, Lord, that we can abide in your peace, even in a troubled world. In Jesus' name. Amen.

Rev. Elaine Beckford

Going Through Samaria

"And he must needs go through Samaria."

-- John 4: 4

Recently, I attended a function with a friend and another friend of hers was also present. At the end of the function, my friend accepted a ride from this friend who lived in proximity to her home. On their way, the driver took a strange route, but my friend did not question her decision. As they drove onto the city streets from the highway, they encountered a woman who was completely covered, exposing only her face and eyes. This woman was going from one vehicle to another asking for money. As she approached my friend's car asking for a few dollars for food, my friend recognized her voice and this stranger recognized my friend's face and shouted her name.

Unexpectedly, she gazed into the eyes of her middle school student from decades ago. This strange encounter presented the opportunity to minister to a young woman who admittedly and undoubtedly had fallen into an addictive lifestyle.

Jesus had to go through Samaria because he had a mission to accomplish. He was about to enter a city that every Jew hated. It was a region of half breed, a mixture of Judaism and Paganism. Jesus was intentional in embarking on this journey. There was a soul waiting to be rescued from the jaws of sinful living. We too must learn not to dwell in such places but to pass through as we fulfill our mission. Whatever is plaguing your city, there is someone there who needs the Lord's attention.

Luke 2: 29 tells us, "I must be about my Father's business." As Christians, we are called to share the good news, even to people in places like Samaria. It was necessary that Jesus go there. His was a rendezvous with destiny because this woman with a checkered past was in search of water that was not in the well.

So often we dismiss and avoid people who are not from our social or religious background, not realizing that they too need a Savior. Romans 3: 23 reminds us that "all have sinned and come short of the glory of God." That includes you, me, and them.

Who in Samaria do you need to reach with love and compassion? People need living water that satisfies their spiritual thirst. My friend's past student needed something that a few dollars could not buy. She needed an encounter with Jesus Christ, just like the woman at the well. Jesus is still in the business of going through to come to where you are. Be open to receive His visit.

Prayer

Father, thank you for coming to where we are to rescue us from a life of sin. Thank you for giving us water that brings eternal life. Amen.

Beverly Coker

Be Transformed

"And be not conformed to this world, but be ye transformed by the renewal of your mind..."

--Romans 12: 1-2.

In one scene of the movie, *Shawshank Redemption,* the star Morgan Freeman, who was in prison for murder is telling a Parole Board reviewing his possible release from prison that he was transformed.

"God's truth," he said. "I am no longer the man I used to be."

Yet, he was still peddling contraband (cigarettes, etc.) to fellow inmates.

In this, there was no real evidence of any inward change in his life. In the scripture (Romans 12: 1-2), Paul beseeched the brethren to be transformed. Simply put, transformation for the Christian means a changed life or a renewed life that no longer conforms to the norms of the world, but to that which pleases God.

God is a Spirit, and they that worship Him must worship Him in spirit and truth (John 4:24). A reminder then of three points regarding the Christian transformation.

1. Transformation is brought about by the mercies of God and not of our own accord. The mercy of God manifested itself ultimately in His provision of Jesus Christ to provide a way back to fellowship with Him after Adam's sin. (Ephesians 2: 13).
2. Salvation is through the spirit and thus starts from the inside and works its way into the soul which is housed by the body. Our bodies become living sacrifices, holy and acceptable unto the Lord.

"Holy" means that we are to be set aside and remain sacred for God's work and seek to be in God's perfect will (See Colossians 1:10).

3. Because we are no longer conformed to the world but of a renewed mind, there should be outward manifestations or indications of our transformation. We want the evidence of the Fruit of the Spirit and the standards laid out in Galatians 5:22-24.

Prayer

Father, I ask for your complete transformation. Make me into your image as I should be. Amen.

JAT

Does Jesus Care? Part I

"Martha, Martha, thou art careful and troubled about many things..."

--Luke 10: 38-42

As women, we are forced to play many different roles and take on numerous responsibilities. Most of us at times experience feelings of being overwhelmed to the point of complaining that life is not fair. Today, we begin by looking at Martha's reaction to having Jesus as a guest in her home. Martha might have been a type A personality, a first-born child with a lot of responsibilities entrusted upon her. Her personality characteristics were that of a nurturer and a caregiver. She inherited those characteristics as her place in life and the world expected her to act her part.

Martha, and her sister Mary each had different personalities and purpose. One was a worshipper; the other was a server. Both were doing what they felt was necessary in order to serve Jesus. Remember, God loves all of us exactly where we are so He can bring us where He intends for us to go.

This day, Martha chose to serve Jesus. That's okay. But is that what the Lord wanted? In our busyness, we need to prioritize so we don't miss out on what's important. Busyness for God should not overshadow our need to be with Him. Martha made her task a priority over Mary's task and perhaps in exhaustion, she cried out to Jesus, in fact, complained, "Do you not care?" God cares about every aspect of our lives, but we must be in alignment with what is important to Him. He sometimes chastens us in love to remind us that He cares.

In reflecting on this passage, did you sense some degree of sibling rivalry, some competition among them? Why do siblings argue? Perhaps Martha was feeling left out, overlooked because her sister had chosen the better part. Let me remind you that God cares about the uniqueness of each of us. Make this a teachable moment where you see yourself and your priorities in life. Jesus still admonishes us to "take my yoke upon you.... for my yoke is easy, and my burden is light" (Matthew 11:29-30).

Prayer

Father, I realize that I have not always given you first place in my life. Help me to know that what's important to you should be important to me. Forgive me for not choosing the better part. Amen.

Beverly Coker

Does Jesus Care? Part II

"Martha, Martha, thou art careful and troubled about many things…"

--Luke 10: 38-41

Jesus made time to visit with friends, in particular, close friends such as Martha and Mary. You don't have to be a Mary or Martha for God to love you. Today, we would like to take a look at Mary's relationship with Jesus, which was probably a more intimate relationship where she longed for His presence.

Mary knew Jesus from a different lens. She might have been the rebellious sister who made a mess of her life and whom Jesus had forgiven much. On this occasion of Jesus's visit, she placed herself in a position of worship. She sneaked in to be with the boys because she didn't want to miss anything that Jesus had to say. This was her way of showing appreciation and sincere gratitude for what he had done for her. It is possible that she had an insight as to what would befall Jesus, so she wanted to bask in his presence and show her devotion to him.

This was Mary's approach to expressing love to her Lord. Mary was so in awe of Jesus that little did she know that Martha saw her as being inconsiderate and possibly was giving her the evil eye. Jesus might have sensed the conflict that was brewing between the two sisters, but tactfully, He told Martha that Mary had chosen the better part. Did Martha seek what Jesus wanted of her, or was that low on her priority list? What did He expect from them? Did He expect hospitality?

He calls us to action. What can we do to show that Jesus cares? Let us put our faith to action and become an example of how He cares. During a recent hurricane in Florida and Texas, I saw vivid examples of neighbor helping neighbor in times of disaster. This can be a cold, callous world, so people need to know that others care. How can you personally show others that you care? Someone is in need of your warmth and caring today. Endeavor to make the world a better place.

Prayer

Father, like Mary, I want to wait at your feet in worship and adoration. Thank you for my time with you. Give me the will to go out and show others that indeed you care. Amen.

Beverly Coker

Under New Management: Part I

"Therefore, if any man be in Christ, he is a new creature; old things are passed away. Behold all things are become new."

--2 Corinthians 5: 17

Have you ever had the experience of going into a store that you had not gone into for a while? As you walk in, you notice that it seems different; the clothes are of a different and better quality; even the employees are more friendly. You wonder to yourself, "What happened? Am I in the right place? Then, you observe a sign that says, "Under New Management."

Becoming a Christian puts us under a new management: the management of Christ. The world sees us differently. We see ourselves through different lens as we gain a new perspective on life. With Christ, our lives are renewed. Renewed people operate by new rules, new motives, and new attitudes. If any man be in Christ, whether Jew or Gentile, black or white, rich or poor, as long as you are in Christ you are considered a new creature. God does not discriminate. God transforms lives into new beings.

Psychiatrists rehabilitate, that's why many keep returning to them for additional treatment. God can clearly change people in a more powerful, significant way than psychiatrists can. God transforms and reforms. He gives a complete overhaul. He performs His acts from the inside.

When Paul met the Lord, he was knocked to the ground only to rise as a new creature. Only God can bring about that degree of transformation. Paul's name was changed from Saul to Paul. New management often requires a name change to fit the new image; however, it is not enough to have a new name. More importantly, we need a new heart, a heart of love compassion, forgiveness, and tenderness toward each other.

Old things are passed away. Let us embrace our new image as a gift from God

Prayer

Thank you, Lord for allowing me to become a new creature. Help me to exhibit this new life before my fellow man. Amen.

Beverly Coker

Under New Management: Part II

"But this one thing I do: forgetting those things which are behind and reaching forth onto those things which are before."

--Philippians 3: 13

You serve a God of new beginnings when you accept Jesus Christ as Lord and Savior. You acquire new thought, new practices, and a new nature. God is a God of second chances. He never gives up on anyone. People might give up on you, but not God. Being under new management results in an attitude change. Instead of destroying, you build; criticizing, you bless; pointing fingers, you become introspective. The woman at the well said, "Come, see a man." She might have gone back to tell her partner, "I can't live with you anymore. I am under new management." What are the old ways that have passed away in your life? Attitude? Anger? Malice? Hatred? Can your Salvation stand up in the light of what Paul writes about in 1 Corinthians 13? Let us conduct ourselves in the spirit of humility, gentleness, patience, love, and forgiveness.

In the secular world, new management might take a look at your medical history to see if they can continue to cover you under their new plan. Do you have a pre-existing condition? Christ Jesus covers you regardless. He becomes your balm in Gilead. Under new management, you become future oriented, more optimistic with a more positive attitude. You learn to forget those things which are behind and press through your circumstances, even those that seem like Giants in your life. Develop a vision of the future. Hope in God.

- Galatians refers to a new creation
- Ephesians: a new man
- Ephesians: a new self
- Revelation: a new nation
- Revelation: a new song

These scriptures all point to newness, the transformed life.

It's all new when we encounter the Master. The woman at the well left her water pot which represented her old self. Forget those things which are behind. Begin to read the new Policies and Procedures Handbook which was given to us by God; this is the Bible. It is our manual to heaven.

Prayer

Thank you, Lord, for allowing me to become a new creature. Help me to exhibit the new life, the transformed life before my fellow man. Amen.

Beverly Coker

Understanding Purpose: Part I

"For it is God which worketh in you both to will and to do of his good pleasure."

--Philippians 2: 13

God facilitates and enables achieving His purpose for our lives. Paul, in his epistle to the Philippians, makes it abundantly clear that it is God who directs all our journey in seeking purpose for our lives. We must accept that our purpose in life is ultimately for His pleasure or use. God not only created us for His purpose and prepares us for that purpose, but He also enables and facilitates our achievement of purpose for our lives.

The Jonah **Call to Purpose** (Jonah 1: 1-2) demonstrates God's enabling and facilitating achievement of purpose. Jonah sought to disobey God and tried to escape to another country (Jonah 1: 3). God allowed a storm to rock the boat (verse 4). The ship's crew identified Jonah as the cause for the storm and dumped him overboard. God orchestrated his rescue by having a great fish swallow him and spit him out alive three days later. God gave him a second chance to achieve or fulfill purpose for his life. Nineveh was saved (Jonah 3: 10). A city of 120,000 was brought to repentance. Jonah's use by God to fulfill purpose demonstrates God's support for us to achieve purpose for our lives.

Sometimes, we think that the battle to achieve purpose is controlled by us and we disobey and complain like Jonah did (Jonah 4: 1-3). Sometimes, situations arise which seem contrary to our expectations, but if God is on the journey with us, we need not worry.

Prayer

Father God, you know my weaknesses, but you have given me strength to overcome. I am alive, Father, and I ask you to help me on my journey to seek your purpose for my life. Amen

JAT

Understanding Purpose: Part II

"I will praise thee, for I am fearfully and wonderfully made."

--Psalm 139: 14

The story was told that at an awards function for doctors, one doctor was being honored for his work in cosmetic surgery. As he went up to receive his award, he broke down in uncontrollable tears and was rushed off stage.

Inquiries later revealed that years before when he was about to start his practice, he had received a vision from God. In that vision, he was directed to go to Africa to work among people disfigured by 'cleft palates'. He had not gone and subsequent was burdened that he had not fulfilled God's purpose for his life. Our normal profession or vocation is generally not the specific purpose God intended for our lives; however, working within our profession or vocation in a specific area in response to God's call is certainly fulfilling God's purpose for our lives.

Our steps are ordered by God. We are fearfully and wonderfully made (verse 14). We are equipped from our mother's womb with traits and characteristics to aid in fulfilling God's purpose for our lives. We may not get the call in a direct vision as this doctor did; however, if we are in Christ, the Holy Spirit working within us directs us toward that specific process.

If we feel the urge or desire to dedicate our efforts in a specific area, this would be the start of finding purpose for our lives. We then need to ask God through fervent prayers if that is a specific purpose He has destined for our lives. Finding purpose is significantly rewarding and personally satisfying beyond just financial gains- it energizes you and stirs your creativity to new levels.

Prayer

Father God, you have given me certain traits, skills, and characteristics and Lord, I want to use them for Your purpose for my life. Lord, help me discern purpose, your purpose for my life. Amen.

JAT

What it Means to be Successful

"And he sought God in the day of Zachariah who had understanding in the visions of God and as long as he sought the Lord, God made him prosper."

-- 2 Chronicles 26: 5

Success is something that all of us hope to achieve. Some yearn for success to the point where they are willing to trample on their fellow man in order to reach this goal.

What is success? In other words, how do we measure success? Could we define success as having money in the bank- lots of it, a good marriage and family relationships, good social connections?

Regardless of how you view success, it always requires us to go a step beyond. To be successful, you cannot accept mediocrity. Countless books have been written on how to be successful, but we often overlook the one book that contains the true secrets of success-the Bible, which shows us the path to success. The Bible tells us of Uzziah who sought the Lord, and as long as he sought the Lord, God made him to prosper. Here lies the secret of success: seek the Lord. His word contains wisdom, guidance, and direction. It's our GPS for a successful life. Success is not measured by the things we possess, but our relationship with God and with man.

Do you want to be successful? Start reading the Word and watch your understanding of life increase. In addition, begin your day acknowledging/abiding in the presence of God. It is essential preparation for success. It will adequately prepare you for the activities and events of the day and will give courage to overcome situations that confront us.

God wants us to prosper physically, emotionally, and financially. As He blesses us, we too can become a blessing. Each of us yearns for success, but in order to become successful, we must build on solid foundation and the determination to rise above the ordinary.

Prayer

Heavenly Father, I ask that through your Word you open my understanding and teach me the path to a successful life. Amen.

Beverly Coker

Work in Progress

"Being confident of this very thing, that he which hath begun a good work in you will perform it until the day of Jesus Christ."

--Philippians 1:6

I have been a follower of Jesus Christ for many years; in fact, since my teenage years. I started with the full assurance of salvation. The work of grace was made complete in my heart. Along the journey, I have had set backs, slipped, and sometimes got distracted. However, God has always given me assurance of His presence that He would not leave me nor forsake me.

If God gave salvation to us when we were alienated from Him, how much more will He give us grace now that we are His children. He will never give up on us. Paul was confident and we should be also that God will continue to work in us, or He will work on us, but He will finish the job He started with us.

Yes, we will encounter failures and heartaches along the way, but He stays with us, and as the Psalms states, "The Lord will perfect that which concerns us" (Psalm 138:8).

We started this journey as clay, raw material that needed to be refined and made into something beautiful. Indeed, we are a work in progress, which will continue until the day of the Lord when we are perfected in Him. So then, because we are a work in progress, we should be less critical of ourselves as well as of others when we do not measure up or display human weaknesses.

It is God who does the refinement, not any one of us. As the mantra declares, "Please be patient, God is not finished with me yet." How true, indeed we are a work in progress.

Ezekiel 36:26: *"A new heart also will I give you, and a new spirit will I put within you."*

Prayer

Heavenly Father, I yield myself to you so you can complete the work you have started in me. Help me to hold out to the end when I shall become like you. Amen.

Beverly Coker

Redeeming the Time

"See then that you walk circumspectly, not as fools, but as wise, Redeeming the time, because the days are evil."

--Ephesians 5: 15-16

Have you ever said to yourself, "Wow, look how fast this week, month, or year has gone by"? When you reflect on how much time has been spent on 'the cares of this world' as compared to the things of God, it may provide a bit of a reality check. It is easy to fall into the day-to-day activities of life: children, school work, even work in the church. Even with all the 'To-dos' of life, we must remember to be doing His will, being spiritually productive. Do not waste one of the greatest gifts God has given us: Time. Where there is time, there is hope! There is an opportunity to make the crooked straight, to right the wrong, to undo the negative 'knots' in our lives. The word redeem means 'to make up for,' 'to make good,' 'to recover,' 'to buy back.' We can literally transform our loss into gain once we have decided to make godly use of our time by walking in His will and purpose for our lives and being obedient to His Word.

> *"To everything there is a season and a time to every purpose under heaven."* Ecclesiastics 3: 1-8.

God has designed each of us with a purpose and for us to live out that purpose to His glory. Our very existence is a threat to Satan. Our purpose is designed to crush Satan's head, to edify the body of the believers, to foster right relationship with God, and most of all, to glorify His everlasting name. God is saying in His Word to walk in your **Divinely Created Purpose** which is in His will. We are Kings and Queens of the Most High. We must know who we are, whose we are, and why we are. If you have breath in your lungs, then there is still an opportunity for you to redeem the time. What will you do?

Prayer

Heavenly Father, help me to be conscious of the seasons of my life and to know that you have a **Divine Purpose** for my life. Help me to seize the time while there is yet time. Amen.

Rev. Kirk Burke

God's Timing

"And he said unto them, "It is not for you to know the times or the seasons which the Father hath put in his own power."

-- Acts 1: 7

God chose us before the foundation of the world to walk us along paths designed uniquely for us. Concentrate on keeping close to him. Jesus will set the pace in keeping with our needs and purposes. God's timing in our lives is perfect and we will enjoy life much more if we believe that He knows the right time to answer our prayer request.

Thank God that He knows what is best for us. Confide in Jesus. Let Him bring us where we need to be. His timing is perfect, but it doesn't always feel that way. Setting timelines and deadlines can only be disappointing as milestone after milestone fall by the wayside unaccomplished. Waiting is hard. God always has a plan for our lives. We get anxious to move to the next step, but God takes His own time and He is never accidental. Be patient. Go to God in prayer. Ask Him for patience and guidance through the waiting season. Wait in hopeful expectation for God to work.

Prayer

Father, I know your timing is perfect. Please, Father, help me to wait patiently on you. Help me to enjoy my life knowing that you are in control. Help me not to be anxious about anything, but in every situation, pray with thanksgiving. God, please reward me with strength to remain hopeful in my waiting. Amen.

Hannah Fevrier

The Thief Cometh

"The thief cometh not, but for to steal, and to kill, and to destroy: I am come that they might have life and that they might have it more abundantly."

-- John 10: 10

Thieves are very destructive. They attack when you are most vulnerable. The thief comes to steal, to kill, and to destroy, but Jesus came that we might have life and an abundant life.

Thieves are very intentional. Their plan is to rob and take whatever you have. The greatest thief is the devil. He will rob you of what God has in store for you; therefore, protect what God has given to you.

Here are some things that you can do to protect yourself from the plan of the devil:

1. *"Therefore, let us not sleep as do others, but let us watch and be sober"* (1 Thessalonians 5: 6). Be aware of your surroundings and where you are heading. This is a dangerous world in which we live.

2. The thief will kill you. Do you know why? The thief does not want any resistance/evidence or to be identified if caught. He will do anything to get rid of you.

3. The thief comes to destroy and that is exactly what the devil wants or intends to do to you. He knows that we can be very useful and profitable in the hands of God. He tries to prevent us from accomplishing our purpose.

The mission of Jesus Christ is opposite from that of the enemy. The devil destroys, but Christ gives life, not just life, but abundant life. Do not throw away this valuable chance of an abundant life. Say "yes" to Jesus today.

Prayer

Dear Jesus. I come to you seeking new life, the abundant life. Thank you for rescuing me from the destructive path of the enemy. Continue to pour new life into me. Amen.

Rev. John S. Murray

GOD'S GOODNESS

God is Good

"I would have fainted unless I had believed to see the goodness of the Lord in the land of the living."

--Psalm 27:13

God wants to be good to us! Life sometimes brings you enough negative circumstances that your concept of God can become jaded. You may come to the point that you start believing that maybe you are the exception to the rule and that God does not want to be good to you.

But I want to remind you today that it is in the character of God to be good. Goodness is in the nature of God. He cannot help himself but be good. No wonder Psalm 107:1 tells us, "Oh, give thanks unto the Lord for he is good, and his mercy endures forever." The reason that we are not enjoying some of the benefits of God is that we have lost our expectancy of God being good to us.

The Bible puts it this way, "As a man thinks in his heart, so is he" (Proverbs 68:19), and I am getting all of today's benefits that the Lord has provided for me. Personally, I want every benefit that the Lord has provided for me on a daily basis. Our good Father extends His goodness to us daily. Receive the goodness and mercy that has been assigned to your life today.

Prayer

Father God, I thank you that you are a good God. Daily extend your benefits toward me and us. I praise you for all your good gifts. Amen.

Rev. Laverne Ramsey

Lower Lights

"Brightly beams the Father's mercy from His lighthouse evermore;

but to us He gives the keeping of the lights along the shore.

Eager eyes are watching, longing, for the lights along the shore.

Trim your feeble lamp, my brother (sister), some poor sailor, tempest tossed,

Trying now to make the harbor, in the darkness may be lost.

Let your lower lights be burning, send the gleam across the wave.

Some poor, fainting, struggling seaman you may rescue, you may save."

--P.P. Bliss

My attention was recently drawn to the concept of lower lights as I sang this old, familiar favorite by P.P. Bliss, the highly acclaimed songwriter associated with the famed evangelist D.L. Moody. Bliss' song was inspired by a story he heard about a ship that was lost as it approached the harbor in Cleveland one night during a violent storm. Having passed the range of the lighthouse's beams, the captain needed the lower lights to bring him safely into the harbor, but the lights had gone out. In the darkness, the ship missed the channel into the harbor and ran aground. Bliss finished the story with this caution:

> "The Master (God) will take care of the great lighthouses, but we must keep the lower lights burning."

Lower lights are those small but important lights along the shore that guide vessels safely to the harbor.

The importance of lower lights cannot be overstated. As Christians, we are God's lower lights. There are people all around us who need the smile we can give, the gesture of friendship, the card of encouragement, the listening ear, the phone call, or any small but important gesture that we can extend to keep needy souls off the shoals.

"TO *US* HE GIVES THE KEEPING OF THE LIGHTS ALONG THE SHORE."

How about you? Is your light shining brightly? Has it gone dim? Or worse still, has it gone out?

"EAGER EYES ARE WATCHING, LONGING FOR THE LIGHTS ALONG THE SHORE."

Without our lower lights, who knows what shipwrecks will happen? As Christians, we are called to be there for others who may be lost on the water needing to make it safely to shore.

"LET YOUR LOWER LIGHTS BE BURNING."

"You are the light of the world"

--Matthew 5:13

Prayer

Father, help me to keep my lower lights burning through which others will see you and come to know you. Amen.

Sheila Hoyte

The Golden Years

"I have been young, and now am old; yet have I not seen the righteous forsaken, nor his seed begging bread."

--Psalm 37:25

This year, I entered another major milestone in my life called the Golden Year or being a Senior Citizen. For years, I denied joining this club until my body forced me to accept reality. I must admit that for so long I secretly embraced my AARP membership card and only used it for my convenience, like getting discounts and other benefits. Little did I know that I was robbing myself of this beautiful season of my life.

These golden years can bring joy, serenity, and fulfilment in one's life. God has blessed me with three score and ten. It's a gift that I no longer reluctantly accept, but for which I graciously give thanks. I am grateful for healing when my body needed to be healed, for wisdom to know when to let go and move on, for the children from whom I have learned so much. Life continues to provide opportunities for growth and renewal.

In reflection on one's life, we can celebrate God's goodness and His mercies towards us. David unashamedly said, "I was young and now I am old, and I have never seen the righteous forsaken nor his seed begging bread" (Psalm 27:25). I am indeed blessed and fortunate to have lived this long to witness God's Hand at work in my life and those around me. I have witnessed miracles, healing, prosperity and abundance. I have seen the sun from different angles, when it was clouded by darkness, seen the midday brilliance and when the glow disappeared at sunset, but always the presence of God abides with me.

As elders, we are in a position to tell our stories to instill values, to see our children and grandchildren go from strength to strength. In Paul's letter to Timothy, he called "to remembrance the unfeigned faith that is in thee, which dwelt first in thy grandmother Lois and thy mother Eunice" (2 Timothy. 1:5). We are carriers of the faith. Our journey of faith is coming to a close. Hopefully, we will be able to say like Paul, "I have fought a good fight, I have finished my course. I have kept the faith" (2 Timothy 4: 7).

How can I close today without reminding you that aging comes with what I consider to be "relatives," such as arthritis? The Lord's wish is that "thou mayest prosper and be in good health, even as your soul prospereth" (3 John: 2). So, take care of your temple. If you haven't started, begin today so you may be able to enjoy a long life ahead.

"For I am with thee, be not dismayed for I am thy God. I will strengthen thee. I will help thee." (Isaiah 41:10).

Prayer

Lord, you have been faithful to me in the past and will be to the end. Thank you for helping me to overcome adversities during my seasons of life. Amen.

Beverly Coker

Lord, Show Us Thy Favor: Part I

"Lord, how wonderfully you bless the righteous. Your favor wraps around each one and covers them under your canopy of kindness and joy."

--Psalm 5:12

Favor is a special kindness shown to us that we do not work for and often do not deserve. Many of us are favored beyond our wildest expectations. When we are shown favor, we in turn should seek to extend favor to others. I have been fortunate to receive favor in my personal and professional life from many whose favor I did not deserve. As a result, I feel obligated to extend favors to others who might be less deserving. When you have God's favor, you will find that people begin to favor you also.

I have been favored to listen to Bill Winston's teaching on "Favor." What a powerful teaching! I would like to share with you some of his key points.

1. Favor opens doors for you.
2. When you have favor, you are divinely positioned.
3. Favor promised to Abraham is also promised to you (Galatians 3: 29).
4. You have to learn how to walk in favor.
5. When you have favor or grace in your life, nothing can stop you, except to win (1 Corinthians 15: 10).
6. Favor determines your destiny (Psalm 102: 13, 16).
7. One encounter with favor is worth a lifetime of labor.

Each day we pray for favor upon our lives in regard to our health, family, jobs, etc. The Lord promises to bless us abundantly, more than we can ask or hope for. That is favor!

When we exercise our faith, favor is granted to us. Joseph received favor and it brought him from the pit to the palace (Genesis 39). Ruth, an ordinary Gentile woman was shown favor which resulted in her marrying Boaz, a wealthy man (Ruth 2: 1). Her name is listed as an ancestor of Jesus. What a favor!

The devil cannot stop God's favor upon your life. God does not discriminate in granting favor to His children. When you are under attack; when your world is crumbling; when you have lost all like Job did, God can still show you favor by restoring what the canker worms have eaten. The Lord promised that no weapon formed against you shall prosper. That is favor!

You might wonder, "How do I access this favor as I am ready for a change of direction?" Simply exercise your faith. All things are possible to him who believes. Favor comes through faith. Don't live a defeated life when God wants to show you favor. Pray for His favor.

Prayer

Dear Father, I am tired of feeling defeated. I am tired of feeling at a loss. Please, show me your Divine favor. I trust you by faith. Amen.

Beverly Coker

Lord, Show Us Thy Favor: Part II

"...for the time to favor her, yes, the set time has come..."

--Psalm 102:13

God has an appointed time to manifest His favor in our lives (Psalm 102: 13). Hezekiah was told he was going to die. He prayed and God prolonged his life (See Isaiah 38: 1-5).

Favor is "demonstrated delight" a state of being approved or held in high regard by another. It's unearned, undeserved preferential treatment. When we favor someone, we want to spend quality time with him or her. We usually favor people who favor us. Another dimension of favor is fellowship. In that context, we are exhorted to nurture our fellowship with God. As our fellowship with God deepens and we delight ourselves in Him, God rewards us with His favor (See Matthew 6: 33).

Having favor does not erase difficulties in our lives. Look at some of the Bible "greats" who experienced both favor and difficulties-Joseph, Noah, Job, Daniel, Mary, and others. It is noteworthy to observe how God showed favor through his protection, provision, promotion, deliverance, and guidance in the lives of these heroes.

God will cause others to be displaced in your favor. This can happen for you. He is your Father-just ask! Many years ago, I had the challenge of dealing with a difficult manager. The Holy Spirit directed me to pray about keeping my spirit clear and to ask God to change *me*. I had no control over my manager's spirit. Fast forward, through a series of events, she was terminated, and I was promoted to take her job. I *KNEW* that was God's intervention! I didn't possess the necessary skill set to handle that level position, but God matured and nurtured me to be successful. That's favor!

It is very important that we do not elevate ourselves as "the source" as though we achieved on our own. As God bestows victories, blessings, and successes on us, give God ALL the glory always for visiting us with His favor!

Prayer

Father, I thank you for your love and faithfulness; your mercies never fail. Help me to minister love and kindness to others and bring honor to your name. Amen.

Monica Case Williams

My Good Shepherd

"O, give thanks into the Lord for He is good."

--Psalm 107: 1

The Lord is my Shepherd. He has been with me through the storms of life. He paid an awesome price on the cruel cross to save you and me. David said, "The Lord is my Shepherd" (Psalm 23: 1), not just my shepherd, but our Good Shepherd. Yes, He is our Good Shepherd because He takes care of us night and day. He is our Provider, our Protector, our Healer. He delivers from temptations. He meets all our needs-yes, He is our Good Shepherd.

Sheep can be very willful, and they tend to wander off without regard for danger. But Jesus knows where to find us. Jesus compares Himself to a good shepherd who intimately knows His sheep, even those who go astray.

"All we like sheep have gone astray; we have turned everyone to his own way" (Isaiah 53: 6).

There is a desire in each of us to be known. As our Good Shepherd, Jesus knows everything about us, yet, He loves us unconditionally. He knows me and accepts me as I am. He is patient, long-suffering, and caring. That is why He is the Good Shepherd. He doesn't judge or condemn us, but always seeks to bring us into His fold. David says, "He maketh me to lie down in green pastures" (Psalm 23: 2). Who could do that but Jesus?

Jesus is the Lamb of God, the Prince of Peace, the Mighty God, but most of all, He is my Good Shepherd. Whether I walk through the valley of the shadow of death, or I am on the mountaintop, He is my Good Shepherd. I will wait on my Good Shepherd and when my life on earth is ended, I will enter into the joy of my rest. How about you? Is He your Good Shepherd?

Prayer

My Good Shepherd, thank you for caring for me. Forgive me for the times when I wandered away. Thank you for leading me with your love and mercies. You are my Good Shepherd. Amen.

Mother Irene Stewart

TESTIMONY

Waiting on the Lord: Part I

"Wait on the Lord; be of good courage."

--Psalm 27: 14

I had brain surgery years ago and I remember I was terrified when I got the news that I had a brain bleed that required surgery. I had two young children and a husband who needed me and whom I deeply loved. I had a career that was just starting to take off, and the thought of leaving all that was scary. I can't really remember how this Bible verse came to my attention, but it became my mantra that I would repeat whenever I was overwhelmed with fear.

Many people find the current state of our country frightening or are facing health challenges or life challenges. Remember that God is in charge and we really have nothing to fear. Trust in the Lord and be of "good courage."

Prayer

Lord, teach us to wait upon you regardless of what we face. Help us not to lose courage when we place our confidence in you. Amen.

Stephanie Lightfoot

Strong Faith

"Whenever I am afraid, I will trust in you."

--Psalm 95: 6 *NKJV*

A gentleman once asked a great man of faith, "What is the best way to have strong faith?" He responded, "The way to have strong faith is to endure great trials." Obviously, not many people would accept that definition. However, when you examine the lives of and work of most of the great achievers of society, you discover that the great hurdles they overcame empowered them. They had to literally lose their own selves to the cause and depend on someone greater than themselves.

Faith is a matter of trust, to relinquish trust in one's self and put that trust in another. Take for example, the story of the woman with the issue of blood in Luke 8: 46-48. She had put her trust in physicians, but to no avail. Now, she put all her trust in Jesus, believing that He could cure her. According to Jesus, it was her faith that made her well. Jesus made the proclamation several times. Friend, you may not realize the value of your present situation, but when you are facing great difficulty, know that it is an opportunity for you to demonstrate strong faith.

Many years ago, *enroute* to work, I stopped at a bank to hail a friend whom I had not seen since I returned from abroad. I was immaculately dressed, walked in, and stood apart from the waiting customers, just watching the flow of their being served one by one. Suddenly, someone grabbed me from behind by my neck. I thought it was my friend just trying to scare me, but when I tried to glance sideways to see who it was, the hold tightened and a coarse sounding voice uttered, "Don't move or you die!"

Out of the corner of my eye, I saw the glint of a gun pressed at my temples. Seeing this, I was brought to the end of my human resources and as I let go of them, I closed my eyes, relaxed, and prayed in my mind, "Lord, take control!" As I let go, the power of the immortal, invisible God faithfully came to my rescue. Within seconds, the man loosened his hold and jumped over the counter into the teller's cage, brandishing his weapon and yelling," Put all the money in this bag!" I then looked around, only to see his accomplice at the entrance of the bank wielding his weapon so that no one could enter or leave the bank.

When they collected all the cash, they locked the bank manager, all the staff, and me in the bathrooms and made their escape. I could say I was in the wrong place at the wrong time, but implicit in the story is an experience of coming to the end of myself, my ability to save or defend myself and transferring that power and ability to someone else: God Almighty, who was and is able to deliver from all evil. *"Great faith must endure great trials."* The scripture is replete with examples of the faithful and people of great faith. Romans 4: 18-19 speaks of Abraham who, contrary to hope, in hope believed, so that he became the father of many nations, according to what was spoken, "So shall your descendants be." And not being weak in faith, he did not consider his own body, already dead (since he was about a hundred years old), and also that of Sarah's womb.

Prayer

Lord, increase my faith. Teach me to trust you, regardless. Amen.

Gus Powell

The Name of Jesus

"God is our refuge and strength, a very present help in trouble."

--Psalm 46: 1

In the year 1986, I was very sick with my kidneys. I was under the doctor's care and was required to take 13 tablets every day for three years. I was in unbearable pain to the point where I asked God to take me. But realizing that my time was in His hand, I backed off and waited on His timing. However, I had stopped taking the medication because I was ready to go home. During that time, I heard a voice say, "Wait until your change comes." I looked around but did not see anyone, so I knew it was the voice of my God. From that day, I began to feel His healing power in my life.

The first thing I was able to do was to sit up by myself. From then on, I was able to take care of my personal needs. I give all the glory and praise to God. The Word of God says, "They that wait upon the Lord shall renew their strength" (Isaiah 40: 31). God has not only renewed my strength, but my complete life has changed. Whenever I get the opportunity, I like to share my testimony and give thanks. *"The effectual fervent prayer of a righteous man availeth much"* (James 5: 16).

I would also thank God for my Pastor and other prayer warriors who prayed for me during my time of adversity.

Prayer

To God be the glory. Great things He has done. Amen.

Kareen Jackson

Is There Anything Too Hard for God?

"Is anything too hard for the Lord? At the time appointed will return to thee, according to the time of life, and Sarah shall have a son."

--Genesis 18: 14

"With men, this is impossible, but with God al things are possible."

--Matthew 19: 26

We must realize and accept that with God there is a season and an appointed time for everything. Having accepted that, I would like to briefly share my testimony.

As the time came for my husband and I to be married, we went in for the usual Gyn physical check. Upon completion, the doctor said to us, "I hope there aren't any plans for children, because you will not be having any." He went on to explain that my womb was three-fourth of the way tilted backward. This would make it virtually impossible to conceive a child. At the time, we were not too alarmed because we wanted to get settled, buy our first home, and then think about children. Having accomplished our plans, now it's time to think about a family. So, the pressure for me to get pregnant was mounting. We visited various civilian physicians and because my husband was now in the military, we are able to go to the best ob-gyn doctors and clinics. Even with the best doctors, nothing was working. All my siblings, friends, co-workers were having babies, but nothing was happening for me.

Turning point for me: I began reading the book *God Will Heal You* by A.A. Allen (now deceased). After reading this book, the Lord gave me a Rhema word. He spoke vividly to me one morning as I was in the bathroom. He said, "I will heal you." Very soon after receiving the Rhema word from God, I had the opportunity of attending a live crusade in Denver, Colorado being conducted by the late A.A. Allen.

When the time came, the altar call was extended. I started down to the altar, but never made it. The Spirit of God over-shadowed me, and I was rolling like a ball down toward the front of the auditorium. A short time after that crusade, my husband became very ill. He was under doctor's care, but nothing seemed to be working. Finally, the doctor at the military base told my husband, he couldn't find anything wrong with him. Having reached their limit with my husband, they suggested that I come in for an examination. My thoughts were, "Why examine me? I am not sick." My husband was the one who was sick.

I went to get examined by the doctor. At the end of my examination, the doctor came out and said to my husband, "I have found your problem." Wonderful, we both thought. The doctor said, "Your wife is pregnant, and you are the one who is having the morning sickness." After my first trimester, my husband was fine and went back to work. I was then three months pregnant. I did not have any of the painful, risky, uncertain surgeries recommended for me. Nine months later, my beautiful daughter was born. At God's appointed time and season, He visited me. With man, this was impossible, but with God, all things are possible. To God be the Glory!!

Prayer:

Lord thank you for your many miracles. Indeed, nothing is

impossible with You. Amen.

Pauline Washington

With God All Things Are Possible

"For with God nothing shall be impossible."

--Luke 1: 37

This is the second time that God has performed miracles for me through His mercy and goodness.

In the year 1998, November 18, my daughter became ill after her appendix ruptured. I was in Canada at a fasting service when I heard a voice say to me that I have to be home by November 29. I told my daughter-in-law and she said, "Mom, I don't think I can get a seat on Air Canada as all the seats must be booked." I told her that one seat is there for me. As it turned out, only one seat was left.

I was able to go home, not knowing that my daughter was ill and was in the hospital. From the Airport, my son-in-law turned off to another road. I asked him where he was going, and he said to the hospital. That was when I knew that my daughter was in the hospital. She was discharged that night. The following day, the devil attacked her again. She was practically dead. When I arrived where she was, I called her name, slapped her face, but no response. Her hand was cold.

A voice told me to speak life in Jesus' name. I called on Jesus to come to our rescue. Then I heard her say, "JESUS," and I told her to call His name again, which she did. Today, she is alive and well and serves as the secretary for her church. My God is mighty, all powerful, awesome, and altogether lovely. We can depend totally on Him.

Prayer

Father, I thank you that You never fail, nor lose a battle.

With you everything is possible. Amen.

Kareen Jackson.

Waiting on the Lord: Part II

"I waited patiently for the Lord; and he inclined unto me, and heard my cry."

--Psalm 40: 1-3

Waiting is never easy. It calls for much patience whether it be the natural, or for something in the supernatural. In Psalm 40, David speaks of "patiently waiting on the Lord" as he cried onto Him. How long he waited for his prayer or prayers to be answered, no one knows. One thing we know is that God "heard his cry." This teaches us that God sometimes does not always answer immediately. However, David encourages that ultimately, He will hear and answer.

What is it that you are waiting on God to do for you? Are you sometimes discouraged and ready to throw in the towel? I exhort you to wait. Don't quit on God. He says, "He will never leave us nor forsake us" (Hebrews 13:5). From personal experience, I can attest to the fact that we serve a prayer-answering God.

My health condition was incurable according to my neurosurgeon. I needed to take medication for life. However, through prayer, fasting and trusting in God, He healed me many years ago so that the doctor actually stopped me from taking the medication. (Jeremiah 32: 27) declares, "Is there anything too hard for the Lord to do?" Psalm 40 says, "He has put a new song in my mouth." Songs of praise will emanate from everyone for victories won through waiting prayerfully on the Lord.

Prayer

Lord, teach me to be patient as I wait on you. I know that you will come through in your time. Thank you. Amen.

GAT

Healing is Available

"But he was wounded for our transgression, he was bruised for our iniquities: the chastisement of our peace was upon him; and with his stripes we are healed."

-- Isaiah 53:5

As human beings, we are all subject to various types of illnesses. However, I have great news for you. Jesus Christ paid the price for our redemption and healing when He died for all mankind. He provided healing for everyone. To be healed, you have to experience some type of illness in your body. We are all broken in mind, body, soul, and spirit. You do not have to remain that way as deliverance is available. Right now, you can receive your healing.

I would like to share with you one of my many experiences of divine healing from the Lord on my journey with Him.

On December 4, 1966, I was rushed to a hospital in Jamaica for emergency surgery. While lying on my back, waiting for the doctor and his team to perform emergency surgery, I took my Bible and read Isaiah 53:5. I remember putting the Bible under my head, closing my eyes, and getting a hold of Jesus Christ. He came to my rescue. I felt when someone touched me. I opened my eyes and saw a nurse who said to me, "I am going to prepare you for surgery." I told her, "Go ahead." I closed my eyes gain and heard her telling her assistant, "Leave him alone. Do not touch him." The doctors came in and did their examination and decided "NO SURGERY."

I cannot show any scars on my body, because Jesus did not leave any. He is real, He is alive. Jesus Christ can heal your body. He healed mine and is waiting to do the same for you.

Prayer

Dear God, please heal your suffering child today, from the crown of his head to the soul of his feet. In the name of Jesus Christ. Amen.

Rev. John S. Murray

Healing

"He heals the brokenhearted and binds up their wounds."

--Psalm 147:3

"My son, be attentive to my words; incline your ear to my sayings. Let them not escape from your sight; keep them within your heart. For they are life to those who find them and healing to all their flesh."

--Proverbs 4:20-22

Sin entered the Garden of Eden to the spoiling of our soul, and the world and "man" in it became subject to brokenness. Because of the work of the Cross, Jesus defeated what was done in the Garden of Eden. The Bible tells us that by His stripes we are healed. But God, not without mercy and an everlasting love for His creation, became our **Jehovah Rapha;** restoring 'health' to all facets of life. (3rd John: 2).

Jesus "transcended that heritage" while on earth. The Bible says, "He went about doing good and healing all." (See Acts 10:38). The Synoptic Gospels covered many a tale of Jesus healing folks; mind, soul and body - the oppressed, the depressed, the brokenhearted, the demon possessed, and the sick in body. Nothing was too hard or too far gone that He could not restore; **He raised people from the dead!** (Matthew 9:18-19, 23-25), (Luke 7:12-15). Through Calvary we are restored physically, mentally and emotionally. What a God!!

LET'S BELIEVE AND BE HEALED

Prayer:

We thank you Lord that, as it was yesterday, the same is

unto today, and we joyfully receive our healing which you have purposed for us through Jesus Christ. (Isaiah 53:5). Amen.

Sonia Brown

Standing on the Promises of God

"For thou, O my God, hast told thy servant that thou wilt build him an house: therefore thy servant hath found in his heart to pray before thee."

--1 Chronicles 17: 25

Many years ago, my husband and I sold our house as we had moved into a company house. There was not any hurry to acquire another one of our own as we were living rent free. My husband thought we should just deposit the money into our savings account. I was not totally convinced that we were doing the right thing, but I trusted the Lord for His guidance.

In addition to my regular daily devotion, I would open the Bible randomly, especially at nights, and meditate on the passage that appears. Well, this night in question, I got 1 Chronicles 17 and the verses that jumped out at me were verses 25-27. I had never seen this scripture before. In it, David was reminding God that He had promised to build him a house. As we recall, the house was built later, but it was built by his son Solomon instead. I applied this Word to my situation and said, "Really God. You are going to build me a house?"

Because of this Word, my husband and I bought a property and built our Dream House almost immediately. Everything went so well, I was confident I had heard from God. 2 Corinthians 1:20 says, "For all the promises of God in Him are yea and Amen onto the glory of God by us." God watches over His Word to perform it. Whatever He says, He will do. He says in Mark 13:31, "Heaven and earth shall pass away, but My words shall not pass away." God has chosen us to bring about His promises on earth.

Let us believe His promises. He is not a man that he should lie.

Prayer

Dear Lord, please forgive us for doubting Your Word. It is infallible. Give us the faith to believe and trust Your Word with all its promises wholeheartedly. Amen.

GAT

RELATIONSHIPS

God of Second Chances

"A certain man had two sons."

--Luke 15:11-32

All of us have wandered away from our Father's house at one time or another. Some have gone too far and stayed too long. Others have stayed home, but mentally have left. The prodigal son is a prime example of one who left the comfort and security of home, but who eventually became cognizant of his predicament and therefore made a decision to return home. He returned home to the arms of a waiting father who embraced him in the spirit of true forgiveness.

This father exemplifies God's willingness to accept and forgive us, regardless of our physical and mental condition. He overlooked the filthiness of his son as his physical condition did not diminish his biological ties to his father. Nothing can break the bond of sonship. Our Heavenly Father is always delighted to accept us when we return from our reckless and wandering ways. He does not remind us of our shortcomings. He does not accept us back with reservation nor does He consider the cost of our welcome. He has proven to be a God of second chances.

Let each of us examine our own ability to forgive. Do we give the people who have wronged us the opportunity to get back in our lives? Or do we remind them that they have blown their chances?

Isaiah reminds us, "For a small moment have I forsaken thee, but with great mercies will I gather thee" (54:7-8). If God who sees the total picture is willing to forgive us of our failures, how much more should we be willing to forgive those who have hurt and disappointed us? God holds nothing against us. What a forgiving Father!! Let us endeavor to welcome back others who have not lived up to our expectations.

Prayer

Father, thank You for Your forgiving spirit. Help me to be willing to forgive others as You have forgiven me. Amen.

Beverly Coker

Intimacy with God

"As the deer pants . . . so pants my soul."

--Psalm 42:1-2

God revealed His acts to the Israelites (distant) but His ways were known to Moses (intimacy) who knew and talked with God (Psalm 103:7). Feeling is an integral component of intimacy. However, feeling is basically conditional; it's an emotion while intimacy is an experience that is personal and private.

Many are content with knowing *about* God; some venture further – busy working for God, like Martha, but Mary chose the *best* part. She sat at Jesus' feet; she hung onto every word He spoke and captured what was dear and precious to His heart. Hear the passion in these verses, "As the deer pants" (Psalm 42:1-2); "He who dwells in the secret place" (Psalm 91:1-2); "That I may *know* Him" (Philippians 3:10 *AMP*). David epitomized having a heart for God. Peter wanted to remain in the glory on the Mount of Transfiguration (See Matthew 17:2-4).

Only the High Priest could enter the Holy of Holies in the Tabernacle, but when Jesus was crucified, God ripped the veil in two, giving us access into the very presence of God Hebrews 4:16. He *desires* intimacy with us, *"They who hunger and thirst . . . shall be filled"* (Matthew 5:6).

How do you cultivate that intimacy? Having a desire, time, and discipline. Read and ***meditate*** daily on His Word, constant prayer and fellowship with the right people. Gradually, your hunger will increase. You'll be transformed as you experience fresh revelation from His Word and experience His glorious presence and love.

Prayer

Father, I desire to know you more intimately. Holy Spirit, illuminate my spirit and give me a passion for the deeper things of God, in Jesus' Name, Amen.

Monica Case Williams

The Union of Marriage

"Therefore, shall a man leave his father and mother, and shall cleave unto his wife: and they shall be one flesh."

--Genesis 2:24

Marriage is a sacred institution that was ordained by God. God's plan before the fall was that in this union, one should be able to find peace, protection, and acceptance. However noble it seems, marriage is not devoid of trials and frustrations. Can two imperfect people come together to make a perfect union? I hardly think so, but with God's blessings and guidance, a couple is able to work through the challenges of marriage.

The agape love, which is the highest form of love, is demonstrated by God to us and from us to one another. A man is instructed to love his wife as Christ loved the church. This form of love requires forgiveness, reconciliation, and restoration.

The Bible gives explicit instruction on the manner in which wife and husband should treat each other. Paul states that we should "submit to one another out of reverence for Christ" (Ephesians 5:21). Submit, is not an archaic word that should be removed from modern day language. It is a reciprocal action in which each puts the other person first, out of love, respect, and devotion.

A wholesome marriage strengthens the individual, the family, as well as the church. The church is as strong as marriages are strong. In today's society, many marriages seem to be in trouble but a marriage that is built on the principles of God's Word will weather the storms. When circumstances arise, too often we lose sight of the vows we initially made and look outside of our marriage for consolation. Let us recommit our marriage to the One who designed marriage, honors marriage, and equips us to love until death do us part.

If your marriage is facing a downward, out of control spiral, there is hope and help available. First and foremost, speak with God, then if necessary, seek professional counsel. A marriage relationship is a beautiful, fulfilling encounter between a man and a woman, but it requires work—work—work. How much are you willing to invest?

Prayer

Our Father, there are many today who are facing storms in their marriage. They might be broken, bruised, and angry. Give them the courage to hear from you again and to be guided by your principles. Amen.

Beverly Coker

He Knows Me

"I want to know Christ and the power of his resurrection and the fellowship of sharing in his suffering becoming like him in His death."

--Philippians 3:10 *NIV*

When we become one with Christ Jesus by trusting in Him, we experience the power that raised Him from the dead. That same power will help us to live a victorious life as we are daily renewed by His power and presence. What an awful death He suffered just for you and me. But as His life was predestined for the cross of Calvary, so are our lives predestined to serve our God. May we be empowered by the resurrected Jesus. We can count on our God that He is able to take care of us.

We will not be defeated by the deceptions and the onslaught of the enemy, because God has everything in His control. The way may be rocky and steep, but as we travel along, His hand will guide us. Sing a song of praise, cry if you may, but be encouraged that our God is an on-time God. Troubles will not last; difficulties will not last because God has a purpose for your life and mine. We raise the banner of hope in God today because He's watching us from a distance.

The song says, "He touch me, oh He touch me, and oh the joy that floods my soul. Something happened and now I know, He touched me and made me whole." Wholeness means that God completes everything in your life, and nothing is lacking. Things may seem dark, but there is always hope beyond darkness. There is always daylight after midnight and so our hope is in an unfailing God because He knows more about us than we know ourselves.

Praise His name.

Prayer

Lord, my heart longs for you. My desire is towards you. I seek your face because I know that my help cometh from the Lord, the maker of heaven and earth. Help me daily that I will get close to you in a remarkable way. Therefore, upon the confidence of your word, I take courage in trusting you daily as I serve you with my whole heart. I wait on you Lord, in Jesus' name. Amen.

Coleene Shaw

Living the Good Life

"He who would love life and see good days, let him refrain his tongue from evil, and his lips from speaking deceit. Let him turn away from evil and do good; let him seek peace and pursue it."

--1 Peter 3:10-11 *NKJV*

Quoting directly from Psalm 34:12-16, Peter gives us the perfect "formula" or prescription for the good life: keeping our tongues from evil and our lips from speaking deceit. Let's not miss the context of this divine instruction: responding to challenging relationships and difficult people—our enemies.

Peter's instruction echoes what is perhaps the hardest thing Jesus said in His Kingdom constitution unveiled in the Sermon on the Mount:

> *"But I say to you who hear: Love your enemies, do good to those who hate you, bless those who curse you, and pray for those who spitefully use you"* (Luke 6:27-28).

Loving and blessing our enemies is the secret door to freedom from the hurts, pain, and trauma of our past. It is also the shortest route to sincerely forgiving someone from the heart. Why? Because it is impossible to speak good of someone and hold ill feelings towards them at the same time.

Do you or someone you know struggle with unforgiveness? Blessing our enemies in not about letting them off the hook. Rather, it has everything to do with launching ourselves into the good life. Speaking words of blessing to and about those who have wronged us actually qualifies us to inherit a blessing above and beyond the gift of the birthright blessing that God has ordained for each of us to have.

> *"Not returning evil for evil or reviling for reviling, but on the contrary blessing, knowing that you were called to this, that you may inherit a blessing"* (1 Peter 3:9.)

Why not unlock your above and beyond blessing inheritance and access to the good life by choosing right now to bless the person(s) who may have hurt you in some way? As Psalm 107:20 says, the Word of God can be sent. So can our prayers and blessings. By speaking this blessing aloud from your heart, you are sending them a blessing.

"[Insert the name] ________________, in the authority of God, my Heavenly Father, and by the power of the Holy Spirit, I bless you into the fullness of God's plan and purpose for your life. May God set in place all you need to become the person He created you to be."

Prayer

Heavenly Father, thank you for showing me your secret to the good life. I receive your grace to speak well of others, especially those who have hurt me. Thank you for your blessing inheritance. Amen.

Rev. Marva Tyndale

Your Pastor Needs Your Support

"And we beseech you, brethren, to know them which labor among you and are over you in the Lord and admonish you. And to esteem them very highly in love for their work's sake."

--Thessalonians 5: 12-13

Some years ago, a new Pastor came to the church where I was a member and part of the leadership team. Some members of the congregation were not happy with him and one actually remarked to my son, "Your father seems to like the new Pastor and support him." My son retorted, "My father has supported every Pastor that has led this church because they were God's choice for that time." When I was told about the interchange by a bystander, I was a pleased father.

In Galatians 6:10, we are encouraged to do good to all men especially Christians. Today's reading 1 Thessalonians 5: 12-13, urges us to honor our leaders as they do God's work. This means spiritually and physically. Here are some words to ponder regarding supporting Pastors.

1. They are God's choice for that particular time and place, but they are humans. When we think they err, do not criticize them. Realize that they too are on a path of growth in "Christ likeness" and pray for them.
2. Pastors have physical and financial needs just like everyone else.
3. Financial help is not always cash. How about helping with chores, which would help to lower their expenses, giving of the produce of your garden.

4. Do not entertain gossip and rumors about them. James 1:26 admonishes us to bridle the tongue.
5. Seek to find positive words from God through their messages and exhortations, remembering that not all messages are meant for you.

We tend to set the bar higher for pastors and religious leaders because we say they should know better. The devil knows that, so he will tempt and attack them harder than ordinary people. Pray for your leaders continuously.

Prayer:

Father, help me to support my Pastor and other leaders and encourage them for their work sake. Amen.

JAT

Treat Others as you Would Like to Be Treated

"Judge not, and ye shall not be judged: condemn not, and ye shall not be condemned: forgive, and ye shall be forgiven."

--Luke 6:37

The Pastor who baptized me had a grandson who was only seven years old when I was in my late forties. One day I said to him, "How come you call to me sometimes and other times you don't?" He replied, "Sometimes you don't notice me too." I was taken aback, but after that, I made it my duty to always greet him.

We all like to be treated well and be loved, but many times we fail to do likewise. However, there are consequences to our actions. There are several reasons we do not treat people well. We deem them as not being worthy and less deserving of good treatment than us. We may have been wronged or think we were wronged by them and we are not willing to forgive. We are also being hypocritical when we see and want to point out faults in other people without taking time to address our own faults. Sometimes, our mistreatment of others stems from envy and grudgefulness.

Whatever the reasons, Jesus teaches that there are consequences. Whatever we sow, we will reap as the Bible tells us. Jesus also points out heavenly consequences in Mark 11: 25-26, warning that if we do not forgive on earth, neither will our Heavenly Father forgive us.

In his epistle to the Galatians (6:10), Paul admonishes us to do good to all men. So, regardless of how we are mistreated and for whatever reasons, as children of God, we are to treat people fairly.

Prayer

Heaven Father, help me to forgive others as you have forgiven me. Create in me a clean heart and a love for others. Amen.

JAT

Matters of the Heart

"So above all, guard the affections of your heart, for they affect all that you are. Pay attention to the welfare of your innermost being, for from there flows the wellspring of life."

--Proverbs 4:23 *TPT*

Do you just long for more of what God intended in your relationship experiences?

The truth is, there has never been a time when sound relationship is more needed, yet also a time when broken relationships abound. Often, under the surface of a well-meaning desire for connection, there remains other real important but unseen matters of the heart that are beneath the surface for most of us. It's a heart that is truly longing to live in love and genuine connections, yet one that is also barred by the stuff/pains of life. This heart is at one and the same time the one presently in connected relationship and the one that desires to have deeper relationship experience.

What remains true through it all, the good and the not so good, is that relationship is not just a life option. Relationship is a deep and abiding need for all of us. That's the way God intended it to be. So, wherever you are on your journey of relationship, whether with self, God, others, or in marriage, there are some important things that will support you to make room ongoing for the kind of relationship experience that you truly desire, that God intended, and that your heart really needs.

1. Are you **Ready? - Do a Heart Check-Up**

Know that your heart will attract whatever is within. Be willing to look within. What are you attracting? Be intentionally willing to become more and more aware of the good, the needs, and the pains of your heart. This will open doors for new beginnings.

2. Let's Get **Set - Remember that the foundation of everything is most important to what you desire and build.**

Every relationship begins with an individual. You are important! Your ability to commune with God as an individual, renew your identity as a royal priesthood in Christ, love yourself, heal and be continually aware is the foundation to doing relationship well.

JUSTIFIABLY OR UNWITTINGLY, YOU MAY BE HOLDING TO UNFORGIVENESS OR LACK OF TRUST.

Know that while this may feel humanly safe, as it keeps us closed from letting in those who hurt, it also chips away at the root of our heart and ultimately closes the door for us to shine out as well. Today, commit again to 'guard the affections of your heart'. It means that you intentionally take the steps to be free, to heal from anything that destroys the relationship foundation that God intended in you. Your safety is found under the shadow of the Almighty. Forgive yourself, forgive someone else, love yourself more consciously, and dare to love others more deliberately again!

Modeling what is good releases the opportunity for more good. Your healing is someone else's as well. Remember, *Love lives where forgiveness and healing live.*

3. Let ***Go - Give what is needed***

Trust that God's got this! When you give as a gift what you need, you release your heart to also receive the divine blessing that God has promised you! Do what you know is good, godly and healthy, not just what you've always done. So, dare today to *"Give generously and generous gifts will be given back to you, shaken down to make more room for more. Abundant gifts will pour out upon you with such an overflowing measure that it will run over the top! Your measurement of generosity becomes the measure of your return"* (Luke 6:38 *TPT*).

Prayer

Father, thank you for the wonderful way that you made me with the need for relationships at the very core of who I am. By the power of the Holy Spirit, I receive grace upon grace to engage in the process that will make room in my heart for the kind of relationship experience you created me to enjoy. In the name of Jesus. Amen.

Andrea Boweya

Toxic Relationships

"Be completely humble and gentle; be patient, bearing with one another in love. Make every effort to keep the unity of the Spirit through the bond of peace."

--Ephesians 4: 2-3 *KJV*

Kevin, who was once my favorite brother, hates me. He seems to take great pleasure in sending negative texts written in the wee hours of the mornings to his "friends" telling them how horribly I have treated him over the years. Mental health issues have clouded and distorted his memories and his lengthy texts reflect there is a problem. Praise God his intention to expose or magnify my faults and flaws has mostly backfired. The relationship with Kevin is toxic and seems irreparable.

When I think of my own dysfunctional family, I am reminded of another dysfunctional family recorded in 2 Samuel 13 that involved three of King David's children: Amnon, Tamar, and Absalom. Amnon was half-brother to Tamar and Absalom. When Amnon first laid eyes on Tamar, he was instantly smitten with her beauty and grace. He did the unforgivable: he raped her, disgraced her and then dismissed her. Absalom waited two whole years before avenging her by having Amnon killed.

Feelings of hatred exploded into violence leaving a permanent crimson stain. King David surely must have been deeply grieved when he saw the results of his own sin being played out so grievously and publicly in his own family.

How are we supposed to react when we have been hurt or misunderstood and a private situation becomes an ugly public spectacle? We live in a time when personal conflicts play out on social media.

As a Christian who is living through a torn and toxic relationship with someone I love, I choose to *not* escalate the situation by pouring gasoline on a fire that is already raging. I will *not* respond with a hateful retort or payback. Rather, I will do these four things: I will ask God to reveal to me my own wrongdoing that I might repent, I will pray for my brother and forgive him. Finally, I will rest in God's peace.

Prayer

Lord, give us the grace to forgive others when we have felt the pain of rejection and hatred. Strengthen us that we may truly imitate Jesus who forgave those who sinned against him. We acknowledge that you alone have the power to restore relationships. I pray that we may walk in humility, integrity, wisdom, and love. Amen.

Rev. Clara Ruffin

STEWARDSHIP

The Blessings of Giving

"Give and it shall be given unto you; good measure, pressed down, and shaken together, and running over shall men give into your bosom."

--Luke 6:36

I am sharing my thoughts about giving a few days before Christmas. Each day on my way to gym, I go by a church with a billboard that reads, "Blessed are those who give without remembering and receive without forgetting." How meaningful this is, particularly at a season when so many give in order to receive.

When we think of giving, we often think of monetary and other tangible factors. However, there are so many other ways we can give that do not include these things. How about giving of yourself, your time, and your talent? The greatest gifts often come from people who have little or no money. They give of themselves with a heart that touches another person. Do not limit yourself by your financial means. All around us are people who could benefit, not from things, but time. Think of the homeless, the single parent who is overwhelmed with childrearing responsibilities, the senior citizen who is lonely and in need of a friend. There are countless ways that you can enrich someone's life with the little that you have.

Paul and Silas at the Gate Beautiful informed the beggar, "Silver and gold have I none; but such as I have give, I thee: In the name of Jesus Christ of Nazareth rise up and walk" (Acts 3:6). This is a beautiful example of using the power of God to meet this man's needs. Too often, we focus on getting and not on giving. Start giving and watch the returns, pressed down, shaken together and running over. I have heard that when you give you receive much more than you gave. It's often not the person to whom you gave, but God and your fellowman bless you with good health, favors, love, and a helping hand when one is needed.

Many of us like to give only to people we love and people who can give back to us. Reframe your approach to giving; don't rob yourself of the blessings you so richly deserve. This year, begin to identify ways by which you can enrich or empower someone. You can make such a difference, not by giving from your bank account, but giving from your heart. So, give and be blessed.

"Every man according as he purposeth in his heart, so let him give, not grudgingly, or of necessity: for God loveth a cheerful giver" (2 Corinthians 9:7).

Prayer

Lord, help me to give as you have blessed me, so I can be a blessing to others. Thank you for your gift to me as I seek to share it with others. Amen.

Beverly Coker

Financial Faithfulness

"Therefore, if you have not been faithful in the use of worldly wealth, who will entrust the true riches to you?"

--Luke 16:11 *AMP*

Finances play a key role in our lives, and this verse tells us that how we manage our finances affects our relationship with Christ.

We are all on a financial journey, and this journey will be based either on the world's view of wealth or God's view of wealth. The Bible contains more than 2,350 verses of Scripture dealing with money and possessions and 15% of everything Jesus said had to do with money. Therefore, it is imperative that we develop a Biblical worldview of how to manage our finances based on the principles of the Bible. As we apply God's financial principles, our lives will be transformed.

Below is a chart that shows the contrast of the world's view of wealth versus God's view of wealth:

World's View of Wealth	God's View of Wealth
Our identity is in our <u>wealth</u>	Our identity is in **<u>Christ</u>**
Money brings <u>security</u>	Our security comes from **<u>God</u>**
Money brings <u>happiness</u>	**<u>Generosity</u>** brings happiness
We strive to increase worldly wealth	We strive to increase **<u>eternal</u>** wealth

Closing Thought

Review the chart and decide which of the two views your financial journey is based on. Is it the world's View or God's view?

Application

Things to do this week as you apply this principle to your life:

- Pray and seek God's help in managing your finances based on the principles of the Bible.
- Memorize Luke 16:11.
- Share with others your understanding of the world's view versus God's view of wealth.

Yvonne Mitto

Giving God What is Precious to You

"And, behold, a woman in the city, which was a sinner...brought an alabaster box of ointment."

--Luke 7:37; John 12:1-6; Matthew 26:6-13

What is precious to you that you can give to the Lord today? The Bible tells us of a woman who was a sinner. When she heard that Jesus was in town, she brought her alabaster box of perfume and poured it on his head. This was a very expensive bottle of perfume, equivalent to a year's salary. This might have been her most precious possession, yet she did not hesitate to pour the entire content on him. Surely, this was an act of love and devotion. She did not just take off the cap and pour a portion but the entire content.

In her spirit, she might have sensed that Jesus was soon to die and be buried so she wanted to be the first to anoint His body and show her appreciation to him. What is He worth to you? To Judas, it was 30 pieces of silver, but to this sinful woman, he was worth everything. She gave Him her all, possibly her life's savings. That's how much she cared about Him. As long as the perfume stayed in the bottle, it wouldn't benefit anyone. By breaking the bottle, she was breaking her connection with the past and was openly confessing her love for the Lord. This was an unselfish act of sacrifice. She needed to be set free from her past actions. Of course, there were critics who felt that this was a waste. Her perfume could have been sold and given to the poor. I suppose Judas was one of those who spoke up, but Jesus rebuked him and said, "Let her alone" (John 12:7). This woman has done a good work, a beautiful thing. Before we criticize those who give their all, what do we have to give? A pittance on Sundays? Let us examine our gift and motive for giving. She gave her all. She gave what was most precious to her. She is remembered and will always be remembered for her sacrifice to Jesus.

Prayer

Lord, I do not have much to give, but the little I have, I give wholeheartedly to you. Please accept my gift of love to thee.

"All to Jesus I surrender, all to Him I freely give."

Beverly Coker

FORGIVENESS

The Route to Forgiveness

"Blessed is he whose transgression is forgiven, whose sin is covered."

--Psalm 32: 1

Sometime ago, I had to act as mediator for a case involving an employee and his supervisor. The supervisor felt that the employee had been insubordinate and demanded an apology, while the employee felt he had been first insulted by his supervisor. The employee apologized saying, "I am sorry for being rude to you, but I will be rude to you whenever you insult me again."

They were unwilling to make a sincere apology to each other, to forgive and move on. David sinned against God many times, but always sought forgiveness in a sincere and contrite manner. Psalm 32 starts with a summation and affirmation by David that we are indeed blessed by a God who will forgive our sins and not hold it against us. However, there must be sincerity in our acknowledgement of our wrongfulness and transgressions.

There are distinct steps the Psalm indicates for us to arrive at David's position:

1. We should not expect God to bless us if we keep silent about our transgressions. On the contrary, our conscience will be pricked and our burdens heavy until we repent (v. 3, 4).
2. We must acknowledge our sins to God and not hide what we did wrong (v. 6).

He is God and sees and knows everything. Acknowledging to Him our wrongs and transgression is owning up that we know and accept what we did wrong in His sight and sincerely seek forgiveness.

3. It is through prayer that we seek forgiveness (v. 6). God will then protect and deliver us from trouble (v. 7). God will go further to show us where we had gone wrong and guide us on the right path.

Those who trust in the Lord can then offer praise and worship God with joyful thanks for forgiveness.

Prayer

Father, thank you for forgiving us of our wrongdoings. Help us to always turn to you with sincerity asking for your pardon. Amen.

JAT

Forgiveness

"Forgiveness is the fragrance that the violet sheds on the heel that has crushed it" - Mark Twain -

"Always pray to have eyes that see the best, a heart that forgives the worst, a mind that forgets the bad, and a soul that never loses faith."

-www.livelifehappy.com-

Wise words indeed!

To overcome the hurts and pains of life, be it emotional, mental or physical, is a hard journey. And - speaking from personal experience - it can become even more difficult if these maladies were inflicted by a **trusted** one; friend, relative, spouse...

The flesh is weakened, the soul is wounded, now giving way for bitterness to set in. Bitterness is a cruel torment of soul! To escape, the soul searches for relief in any which way that it can. But relief will not come until the **ROOT** of unforgiveness is doused, plucked up, and destroyed.

Believers to that end, we **must** firmly adhere forgiveness the way God intended it to be so that we can be set free in mind, soul, and body from the offense and wounds which may have been inflicted upon us.

Jesus is our finest example. He forgave our sins. He cried out on the cross, "Father, forgive them for they know not what they are doing."

- **Colossians 3:13**
- **Ephesians 4:31-32**
- **Mark 11:25**

- **Matthew 6:14-15**
- **1st John 1:9**

Prayer

Our Father, we thank you that you forgave us our sins through Christ Jesus. Now, teach us to forgive likewise, when we have sinned against each other.

Sonia Brown

FAITH AND HOPE

Faith

"Faith is the substance of things hoped for."

--Hebrews 11:1 *NIV*

"And without faith it is impossible to please God..."

--Hebrews 11:6 *NIV*

"In accordance with the measure of faith God has given you."

--Romans 12:3 *NIV*

Abraham (husband of Sarah) is renowned in the Bible as the father of faith. He had a firm belief in God and God requited unto him Salvation (Genesis 15:6). God also called him friend (See Isaiah 41:8). WOW!! Such honor.

His name is listed among the greats in the '**Hall of Faith**' (Hebrews 11:8-19) as testimony of a life well lived by true faith in God.

It is our faith through grace that lifts us up to God. No matter the many obstacles or challenges we may face, valleys to cross, or mountains to go over, it is our faith activated, that can and will indeed move those mountains (See Mark 11:23).

My desire is to please God, in living by faith. Who among us would not want to be called friend of God? Or to be lavished with the scriptural terms of endearment:

> 'This is my beloved [your name] in whom I am well pleased (Matthew 3:17).

Simply put, Jesus says, "Have faith in God."

Prayer

Awesome God, Author and Finisher of our faith, we thank

thee with all our hearts. Help us to stand strong like with the Abrahamic kind of faith.

Sonia Brown

Exercising Faith

"Now faith is the substance of things hoped for, the evidence of things not seen."

--Hebrews 11:1

What is faith? Faith is believing what we cannot see. It is holding on to the promises of God that what He says He will do. It is often a misunderstood word because we exercise faith every day in "inanimate objects" such as a chair. We have faith that at the end of every two weeks we will receive a paycheck. However, it is our faith in God that makes all things possible. He determines the outcome of every situation. Faith is putting our total confidence in a God who sees all things.

The author of Hebrews so beautifully refers to people who lived by faith and who died in faith, some without seeing their promises fulfilled. Despite the hardships that many encountered, they never lost their faith. That is the reason why their names can be recorded in the book of faith. Bill Winston, a spirit-filled preacher, encourages us to start in faith, stay in faith, and finish in faith. To get to the finish line, we must persevere in faith.

Try to imagine Abraham, hearing a voice and not seeing anyone - declaring He is God, telling him to leave his established home and family and go to a land – unchartered territories that He would show him. Abraham, in obedience, left by faith. He got revelation as he journeyed, so his faith continued to grow, and he became great - the Father of many nations.

Faith is having confidence in what we do not see. Faith in God will bring us through the most difficult seasons of our lives. Regardless of the clouds that obscure your vision, hold on in faith and don't give up because God will bring forth light out of darkness.

Faith will allow you to be victorious, "so don't lose your bold, courageous faith, for you are destined for a great reward" (TPT).

Prayer

Father, help me to trust you even when I cannot see your hand at work. I put my faith in You that You will work all things for my good and Your glory. Amen.

Beverly Coker

There is Still Hope

"If in this life only we have hope in Christ, we are of all men most miserable."

--1 Corinthians 15: 19

This week, I learned of the passing of a dear friend. I had known her for over 40 years and had spent many beautiful moments with her. Towards the end, I had begun to lose hope that she would be completely healed in this life. I continued to pray in faith hoping for a miracle. God, who undoubtedly understood my ambivalence, chose not to heal her in this life, but make her completely better in the next.

Hope is a means of bringing comfort and peace. However, as we evaluate the present conditions of the world, we tend to lose hope. To maintain hope is this world is difficult when the heart of man is deceitful and so desperately wicked. To find hope in our personal life is difficult when we grieve, when we face illness of one sort or another, when we face challenges that seem unending. Life's problems erode hope.

(Psalm 42: 5) *"Hope thou in God."*

He removes the shadows and gives us a ray of light to hold on to. Any situation has the potential to change, if we hold onto hope. Hope gives us the assurance that today will be better than yesterday and tomorrow the sun will shine again.

As I reflect on my relationship with my dear friend, it gives me hope that this is not the end of this journey. She cannot leave without God's assurance that we will meet again. Today, I grieve with hope that "God will wipe away the tears from our face"(Isaiah 25:8). It is the love for my friend that makes our parting endurable and my grief consolable.

Prayer

Father, I hope in Thee. Help me not to lose confidence in your ability to make changes for the better. Amen.

Beverly Coker

Biblical Hope

"We have this hope as an anchor for the soul, firm and secure…"

--Hebrews 6:19 *NIV*

The story is told of a nineteen-century British painter whose name was George Fredrick Watts, who pictured "hope" in one of his works of art. He painted a woman sitting on a globe of the world playing her harp. Every string on the harp was broken except one. To the natural eye, this looked like despair, but Watts titled his painting "Hope." Watts knew that as long as one string remained, there would be hope of making music from it.

Biblical Hope is heart-felt expectation based on the promises of God. Hope conquers doubt. Hope produces a present reality of the authority and power of God to fulfill His promises. If you live in hope, you will not die in despair.

The times in which we live create an atmosphere of hopelessness. Everything around suggests losing your grip on life, losing sight of hopes and dreams like the woman in Watts' painting who lost all but one string on her harp. You may think you have lost all and the direction for your life is over. But never give up hope! Mark 5: 35-36 tells of a ruler whose daughter was dying. He sent for Jesus, and before Jesus got to the house, hope was lost; the daughter had died. Jesus said to the ruler, ***"Be not afraid, only believe."***

A promise from Jesus gives hope. Anchor your hope in Christ Jesus. He is the Omnipotent One. His promises remain firm. Therefore, rest assured with patient expectation that hope, the anchor of your soul, will remain. Hope is never lost when you believe. Keep your hope alive.

Prayer

Lord, in the midst of trials, keep my hope firm and secure in your love. Amen.

Rev. Lenore Kidd

Hope During the Pain

"And the Lord turned the captivity of Job, when he prayed for his friends; also the Lord gave Job twice as much as he had before."

--Job 42:10

During this life, we were never promised a rose garden. We were never promised that things would be perfect. When the difficult times come, we feel as if we are groping around in darkness. We have such a hard time finding God and His will for our lives during these trying times. I'm reminded of Job who had it all, then one day it was all gone. The situation was so grim that his wife told him to curse God and die. His friends also wondered at his calamity in disbelief. Job was in such despair that he himself wondered why he did not die from the womb or at birth. Job never thought his situation could get better.

Do you feel like Job today? Do you feel like the Everlasting Father, the Almighty God, the Prince of Peace has forgotten you? Well, He has not! God trusted Job to be faithful. Even though Job's friends were not supportive and did not encourage him, God told Job to pray for his friends. God blessed Job with twice as much as he had before. God gave Job double for his trouble. Is God asking us to take our eyes off our situation? Job encouraged us when he said, "All the days of my appointed time will I wait till my change comes." Every tear that you cry is being bottled by the Lord. He did not give us a spirit of fear, but of power and of love and of a sound mind. So, hope during these difficult times, during the pain, for your change is on the way.

Prayer

Father, in the name of Jesus, I pray that You will be our source of strength, joy, and restoration in our times of pain, grief, and despair. Father, please restore double for our trouble, dry our weeping eyes and mend our broken hearts, in the name of Jesus. Amen.

Donna Wilkinson Maxwell

Having Faith in God

"And all things, whatsoever ye shall ask in prayer, believing, ye shall receive."

--Matthew 21:21

Faith is the substance of things hoped for and the conviction of things not seen. Mentally, put God first. Starting at the beginning of your day, practice communicating with Him throughout the day and focus on Him.

Faith does not have to be huge; it just has to be present. If you have faith like a mustard seed, nothing will be impossible for you. Jesus said, "Whatever you ask for in prayer you will receive just have faith" (Matthew 21:22). There is only one path to salvation; we are saved only when we make the choice to put our faith in Jesus. When circumstances and situations around you threaten to pull you down into deep waters of doubt, just ask Jesus to help you to focus on Him and give you a clean and pure heart and greater faith to trust Him.

Prayer

Jesus, please forgive me for my lack of faith. Increase my faith in Your Word and help me to trust You enough to follow Your leading. Give me the faith I need to believe and may my faith in You grow stronger and deeper each day. Please Jesus, bless me with faith beyond comparison. Amen.

Hannah Fevrier

Radical Faith

"Now, a certain man was sick, named Lazarus, of Bethany, the brother of Mary and her sister Martha."

--John 11:1

There are lessons we can learn from Lazarus who was first introduced to us as being sick. Yesterday, in his sermon, my Pastor gave a moving lesson on radical faith. Radical faith applies when the bottom falls out of our dreams. You cannot have radical faith until you've exhausted all reasonable solutions.

To the believer, it is unwavering confidence that even in a bad situation, God is still God and he will come through for you. Roman 8:28 reminds us that God is still in control. God never leads you where He cannot keep you.

Lazarus had a relationship with Jesus. Some people only turn to God when they are in a crisis. How can we go to someone when we are in trouble, if we never spent time building a relationship with that person? Lazarus and his sisters were close friends of Jesus, so when Lazarus became sick it was natural that they call on their friend, Jesus.

As long as you believe you can handle your situation by yourself, you will not come in desperation to God. David said, "I will lift up mine eyes unto the hills from whence cometh my help" (Psalm 121: 1). When you exercise radical faith, you get radical results.

Jesus performed a radical miracle by raising Lazarus from the dead. It had never been done before. Prior to this, Martha had "if only" faith, but as she faced Jesus, she felt that "but even now I know that whatever You ask of God,

God will give you (verse 22). Martha went from "if only" to "even now" faith. Radical transformation! You never know the possibilities of your faith until your back is against the wall. The Shunammite woman looked into the face of her dead son and told Gehazi, "It is well' (2 Kings 4: 26). Radical faith is choosing to take a leap of faith that might cost you something.

Abraham showed radical faith when he went out not knowing where he was going. By faith, radical things happened to Abraham as well as to his wife, Sarah. We too can see radical things happen in our lives when we step out in faith and trust the one who never leads us into insecurity without providing Himself as security. How is your faith?

Prayer

Lord, I thank you that through faith I can experience extraordinary things in my life. Amen.

Beverly Coker

Biblical Christianity

"Jesus answered him, 'Truly, truly, I say to you, unless one is born again, he cannot see the Kingdom of God'."

--John 3:3

It is my observation that the word "Christian" has been used incorrectly and as a label, attached fraudulently. There are many who are acquainted with the church, but they have not been introduced to Christ and furthermore entered into a personal relationship with Him. As the question has been poised before, every "believer" should ask themselves, "If Christianity was a crime, would there be sufficient evidence to convict me?" This cannot be a case of guilty by association. For any guilty conviction to be held up in a court of law, there must be enough evidence presented to support that decision.

Biblical Christianity calls for evidence, change from the old sinful lifestyle to the new way of life. Jesus' word to Nicodemus in St John 3:3 was not a careless suggestion, no; this was an uncompromising requirement to see, enter, and realize the Kingdom of God. There is a required action to receive an unexpected result. In this case "born again" is the required action and the result, "to see the Kingdom of God."

There must be a point in a person's life when they recognized the seriousness of their sinfulness and be willing to change; that is conviction. They must then, turn to God and accept the provision that He has made available through Christ's death on the cross; the payment for their sin; that is conversion. Furthermore, they should be willing to walk in the ways of the Lord as revealed in scripture; that is Biblical Christianity. There has to be a clear distinction of change.

"Therefore, if anyone is in Christ, he is a new creation, old things have passed away; behold al things have become new."

(2 Corinthians 5:17 *NKJV*)

Prayer

Father, thank You for sending your Son Jesus to die in our place so we could become children of God. Help us that we may live Christ-like lives to honor You and be followers of Christ indeed. Amen.

Rev. Charlton Daley

Nothing is too Hard for God

"Is there anything too hard for our God?"

--Genesis 18:14

To the question asked, "Is anything too hard for the Lord"? the obvious answer is, of course, "No!" Nothing is too difficult when we believe in Him enough to go forward, doing His will and letting Him do the impossible for us. Even Abraham and Sarah could have blocked God's plan if they had continued to disbelieve.

This question reveals much about our Creator, God. I, therefore, admonish all believers to make it your duty to insert that specific needs into the question. Is this trial in my life too hard for the Lord? Is this habit I'm battling with too difficult for the Lord to handle? Is the communication problem I'm having too hard for Him?

Asking the question this way reminds us that God is personally involved in our lives and nudges us to ask for His power to help in every situation.

The only thing that will be "too hard for the Lord" is our deliberate and continual disbelief in His love and power, and our ultimate rejection of His plans for us. Nothing is impossible for God to do for those who will trust Him.

Prayer

Father, I believe in You and Your Word. Help my faith to grow as I enlarge my knowledge of You as my faith-object.

Rev. Terry D. Joseph

I Trust You, Lord

"Nothing in all creation is hidden from God's sight. Everything is uncovered and laid bare before the eyes of him to whom we must give an account."

--Hebrews 4:13 *NIV*

TRUST IS THE ABILITY TO CONFIDE WITH FIRM BELIEF THAT THE TRUTH RECEIVED IS TRUSTWORTHY.

Nothing can be hidden from God's sight. He knows about everyone, everywhere. Everything about us is wide open to His all-seeing eyes. Even when we are unaware of His presence, He is there with us. God gives us His Word which was written by inspiration from the Holy Spirit. We can depend on His Word that whatever He says will come through. If He says you are healed then you are healed, if He tells you that He will provide, then He will provide, that's the confidence we have in Him, the God of all creation.

Sometimes life can be overwhelming, but we have to trust God even when there is so much turbulence around us. God cares so much about us. The battles and the journeys before us are uncertain, but we can depend on our God to take us through. Many times, He gives us a directive but does not tell us what will happen between the process and the promise. We have to be open to trust our God because He cannot and will not fail. There is never a moment that we call upon God and He is not there. He has His angels all around us; therefore, let us hold unto confidence knowing that our Father knows where we are and what we are going through. Diseases are on the rise; many persons are receiving unexpected diagnoses, but did you know that God is the ultimate healer? He is the author and finisher of our faith and nothing takes Him by surprise. Therefore, my brother and sister, let us trust God with our whole heart.

Prayer

Father, give me the grace that I need to trust You more. I know that Your everlasting arms are strong around me. Therefore, I take courage in trusting You. Help us to put our trust in you, dear Lord. We ask these mercies, in Jesus' name. Amen.

Coleene Shaw

How is Your Patience?

"Knowing this that the trying of your faith worketh patience."

--James 1:3

Patience is a virtue that more of us wish we possessed. James says the trying of our faith works patience (James 1:3). My faith is always being tested by people who do not possess this fruit of the spirit.

When we drive our cars, we must wait patiently on the highway for traffic to proceed. As commuters, we must wait for the next bus to arrive. Much of our lives is spent waiting, yet many of us have not learned the value of patience. James admonishes us to "count it all joy." It reminds me of farmers who spend much time waiting for their crops to yield. They do not complain because they know that waiting patiently is a part of the process.

The next time we become impatient because we cannot control what's going on **around** us, let's try to control what's happening **within** us. As a pregnant mother waits for the arrival of her newborn, so we patiently wait for the fulfilment of our destiny. Waiting is hard; it's labor intensive, but the results could bring joy.

Have you been waiting on God for something and it seems He is silent or is taking too long? In the interim, God might be teaching us the valuable lesson that He is never late but always on time. Don't be like the person who asked God to give him more patience, NOW!

The gift of exercising patience reveals who we are as a people. It exhibits character traits such as endurance. How much can we endure, or are we inclined to give up and drop-out? Life itself is likened to a race. For some, it is a long race. The Bible urges us to endure to the end, despite life's adversities, trials, and testing. We experience a reprieve now and then, but before long, we are back to being tested. James says," Let patience finish its work so that you may mature and complete with nothing lacking" (verse 4).

Through the experience of waiting, we become more like Christ. We learn to wait, trust, and rejoice in Him.

Prayer

Lord, I ask for patience to endure whatever life brings. Help me to endure knowing that patience produces qualities that I need to possess. Amen.

Beverly Coker

Outward Appearances

"Whose adorning let it not be that outward adorning of plaiting the hair, and of wearing of gold, or of putting on of apparel; But let it be the hidden man of the heart."

--1 Peter 3:3-4a, *KJV*

I squinted as I looked at my reflection. My nose almost touching the smooth surface of the mirror, I peered at the fine lines that gathered at the corners of my eyes, and in my opinion, there was nothing remotely funny about my "laugh lines." I sighed as I looked at the horizontal lines that creased my brow. Can you relate?

In our present culture, we are besieged with products that boast that they will reverse the ravages of age on a monthly basis if we are willing to pay. Several beauty products are touted as miracle solutions to get rid of wrinkles, bags under one's eyes, and uneven complexions. If someone wants a more lasting result, there is always plastic surgery, but even that fails.

Proverbs 31:30 says "Favor is deceitful, and beauty is vain: but a woman that fears the Lord, she shall be praised." Did you get that? It says beauty is *vain*.

Our character, humility, submission to God's will, and our deep and abiding love for the people, purposes, and things of God are what makes us beautiful. Samuel was given the task of anointing the king who will replace Saul. He was not given the identity of the person. He was only told not to judge according to his appearance, "For God sees not as man sees, for man looks at the outward appearance, but the LORD looks at the heart" (1 Samuel 17:7).

Some of the most beautiful women I have ever seen would not win an award for their beauty. Nor are they consumed with their outer appearance. They love the Lord and because of it, they exude a beauty that is unsurpassed. Our concern should be not on the outer appearance only, but on Him who makes us beautiful.

Prayer

Lord God, I come to you in the name of Jesus. Thank you for the lines of wisdom that grace my face and for life itself. Grant me this day to exhibit your wisdom and love to all I encounter. Help me to focus on what matters to You, Your plans and purposes. Amen.

Rev Clara Ruffin

I Believe

"Now if we be dead with Christ, we believe that we shall also live with him."

--Romans 6:8

Recently, I have been examining my beliefs in an age when people are losing faith in their very existence. Someone once said, "If you don't stand for something, you will fall for anything." Here are some of my beliefs that have helped shaped my life:

I believe that Jesus Christ died, was buried and rose again… I believe that the Bible is the infallible, inspired Word of God… I believe in life after death… I believe that the church is under the attack of the enemy… I believe in the true demonstration of God's love towards us and to each other… I believe we are fearfully and wonderfully made… I believe that God created the heavens and the earth and no one can add to it… I believe that there is more to life than what we see and experience…I believe that my life matters and I can influence the world in a positive way…I believe one of these days death will come to each of us… I believe I am ready…I believe that what we sow we will reap. What we give will be returned to us…I believe that God sent His son that we would not perish.

I believe that the family is a divine institution created by God for the continuation of life… I believe in you my brother, my sister, my fellow travelers. We are on our way to Somewhere… I believe there is a hell and a heaven. The time to choose is now…I believe that despite life's challenges and hardships we can still experience joy… I believe that God is fair, impartial and just… I believe in children. They are our hope for the future... I believe in the second coming of the Lord... I believe there is a purpose for each of us. Let's find that purpose... I believe the earth was created for us to enjoy. Let us not destroy it... I believe in faith, hope, and love, but the greatest of these is love... I believe that soon and very soon we are going to see the King.

Our beliefs should make us accountable and propel us into action. How about you? How do your beliefs affect others for God's Kingdom?

Prayer

Father, help me to hold on to my beliefs that have helped to maintain me through life's changes. Most of all, I believe in You. Amen.

Beverly Coker

Why Do We Doubt?

"O thou of little faith, wherefore didst thou doubt?"

--Matthew 14:31

When we pray, God wants us to come in faith, believing that He gives us the desires of our hearts. (John 14:13) Jesus said, "Whatsoever you shall ask in my name, that will I do that the Father may be glorified in the Son." We should not doubt, only ask believing in Jesus's name.

The author of Psalm 106 mentioned the terrible sin that Israel had committed against God by doubting Him. They forgot about the signs and wonders, the miracles God brought about by the demonstration of Moses in Egypt. When they came to the Red Sea and there was no way out, they panicked, forgetting the previous miracles, doubting that God can make a way through the sea. What God did yesterday, He can do today and tomorrow. He is the same God forever.

The signature song of a fellow church member is, "He'll do it again. We may not know how, we may not know when, but He will do it again." Doubt is an enemy; it causes us to lose out on our blessings and promises from God. Personally, I have tremendous faith for others, but when it comes to myself, I doubt. I was like the Israelites; I forgot what God did for me in the past.

In 1992, while my son, David was in the Navy, he sent money for me as I had encouraged him to send money home for his savings account. I saved it in liquid CDs because he could withdraw it at any time. After he came home, we went to the Credit Union to get a loan to purchase a new car. I told the manager that I would not stand surety for him, but I would make sure the Credit

Union gets its money. We pooled our resources and within the year by the grace of God, it was paid off. The manager remarked, "Are you serious?" I said, "I told you."

When it was my time to ask for a loan, I began to ask, "What if?" What if I lose my job? What if my credit gets messed up? On and on I went. Fear got a hold of me. A reminder that when God worked His miracles at the Red Sea, the waters dried up and they were saved. How could they doubt or mistrust God after seeing those miracles? We too act in the same manner when we see no way out. Remember, whatever we ask in Jesus's name, He will do it, so, **do not doubt.**

Prayer

Father in Heaven, help us to come to you in faith, believing that what we ask of you, it will be granted. Help us to trust you completely, never doubting. Amen.

Dorothy Rowland

Trust God

"Trust in the Lord with all your heart and lean not on your own understanding. In all your ways acknowledge Him and He shall direct your paths."

--Proverbs 3:5-6 *NKJV*

This is a very familiar Scripture that many people, including myself, have memorized. We quote these verses frequently, but do we apply them in our lives? Webster's Dictionary defines trust as "to rely on, to place confidence in, to hope or expect confidently." In today's society, it is very difficult to trust anyone. When we hear someone say, "Trust me," we get very skeptical. However, these verses remind us that we must trust God with all our heart.

What does it mean to "trust in the Lord with all your heart?" Picture for a moment, a little girl trying to take her first steps. Just a few feet away is her dad with his arms wide open encouraging her to come to him. The same way, God's arms are wide open, and He is encouraging us, His children, to come to Him and trust Him. I know it may be challenging for many of us to take that step. You may think, "I have trusted individuals in the past and they have let me down." That may be true but know that our God will never let us down.

God wants us to surrender everything to Him, both the good and the bad. He wants us to trust Him in every area of our lives, and we should do so with all our heart because God will never fail us. We must acknowledge God in all our ways and allow Him to direct our path. As we begin to trust God and rest in Him, we will enjoy our daily walk with Him.

Closing Thought

Do you trust God in every area of your life?

Application

Things to do this week as you apply this principle to your life:

- Think about areas of your life in which you need to trust God, and begin to do so.
- Memorize Proverbs 3:5-6.
- Share with three people at least one area you will begin to trust God with.

Yvonne Mitto

Faith Defeats Noisy Negatives

"Yet this I call to mind and therefore I have hope: because of the Lord's great love we are not consumed, for His compassions never fail. They are new every morning, great is your faithfulness."

--Lamentations 3:21-23 *NIV*

Life is filled with a gamut of experiences: ups, downs, joys, sorrows, successes, and failures. No one escapes experiencing life's maladies. Solomon said, "Time and chance happens to us all" (Ecclesiastes 9:11b). Prophet Jeremiah, God's chosen before birth, faithfully served God, yet he encountered trials and tribulations: was ridiculed, mocked, laughed at, rejected, and endured physical ailments. He felt abandoned by God and found himself gripped by depression, loneliness/isolation, and hopelessness. I believe you and I can relate to Jeremiah's feelings of abandonment by God when life hurts so much. It seems so unfair and God's promise "never leave you neither forsake you" (Hebrews 13:5) seems elusive.

When life hurts and faith in God's promise is challenged by ugly realities: sickness - loneliness, or whatever maladies life presents, remember God is faithful. Boldly challenge your present reality with your past experiences of the faithfulness of God. Jeremiah did just that. However, after listening to noisy negatives, he silenced and defeated them by calling to his remembrance personal experiences of God's faithfulness.

Prayer

Dear Lord, thank you for loving me and for your faithfulness, never leaving me alone. Forgive me for succumbing to doubting your presence with me when life is overwhelming. Oh, what joy floods my soul, as I reflect upon your divine intervention in past situations that I have experienced which could have destroyed me. You caused me to triumph and in the midst of turmoil, you gave me peace. Help my heart to always speak words of testimony, proclaiming your mercies are new every morning and great is your faithfulness. Amen!!

Rev. Cecilia Young-Williams

Choose Your Perspective

"Although the fig tree shall not blossom, neither shall fruit be in the vines; the labour of the olive shall fail, and the fields shall yield no meat; the flock shall be cut off from the fold, and there shall be no herd in the stalls: Yet I will rejoice in the Lord, I will joy in the God of my salvation."

--(Habakkuk 3: 17-18

PERSPECTIVE! I woke up with this word on my heart one morning. Immediately, the circumstances of a particular friend flashed across my mind. Usually, that is a call to pray for that person, but in that particular moment it gave me perspective.

PERSPECTIVE! A proper view and true understanding or the relative importance of one thing over another. A particular point of view. A frame of reference.

PERSPECTIVE! Like Looking back as the Red Sea closes over your enemies or at the fallen rubble of the Jericho wall at your feet or at your Haman hanging from the gallows or at Quail and Manna miraculous in your hand when previously there was nothing but air or your prison door busted open - freedom now your choice to take!

A PERSPECTIVE that produces SIGHT!

A PERSPECTIVE that produces FAITH!

A PERSPECTIVE that produces THANKSGIVING!

A PERSPECTIVE that allows us to stand and live from the MORNING of our situations and not the NIGHT!

What perspective will you choose?

Though the fig tree does not bud and there are no grapes on the vines; though the olive crop fails, and the fields produce no food; though there are no sheep in the pen and no cattle in the stalls, yet I will rejoice in the LORD. I will be joyful in God, my Savior. The Sovereign LORD is my strength; he makes my feet like the feet of a deer; he enables me to tread on the heights. (See Habakkuk 3:17-19).

Prayer

Thank You, Lord, for allowing me to see things from Your perspective. Your perspective brings new meaning and insight into my life. Thank You Lord!! Amen.

Minister Alicia Morgan

Cast Not Away Your Confidence

"So do not throw away this confident trust in the Lord. Remember the great reward it brings you!"

--Hebrews 10:35 *NLT*

My husband and I marvel at our grandchildren as they interact with us. They have complete confidence that if Papa James and Grandma have made them a promise, we will fulfill it. This confidence has been reinforced as we have demonstrated our love. The two younger grandchildren believe that all is well when they are in Papa James' presence because he is strong and loving and only wants what's best for them.

This is the same trust that the writer of Hebrews expresses. He reminds the believers that he realizes they have experienced many trials in their Christian walk, yet he encourages them to "... hold tightly without wavering to the hope we affirm, for God can be trusted to keep his promise" (verse 25). What an encouragement!

The writer then asked the believers to reflect on the difficult circumstances they have endured and how they have "remained faithful, even though it meant terrible suffering" (verse 32). They were exposed to horrendous treatment, yet they, "... accepted it with joy." He emphasizes that not only did they prevail through their struggles, but they endured joyfully because they knew something better awaited them.

Finally, the writer admonishes the Christians, "So do not throw away this confident trust in the Lord. Remember the great reward it brings you!" (verse 35). Although we may suffer, we do not cast away our confidence, because there is a great reward of eternal life for those who refuse to "turn away from God." Therefore, we can have the same childlike trust as my grandchildren because God is faithful to keep His promise. Amen.

Rev. Lillian Turnipseed

God's Faithfulness

"I will never leave you nor forsake you" (Hebrews 13:5). "....my grace is sufficient for you, for my power is made perfect in weakness."

--2 Corinthians 12:9

From Genesis to Revelation, the living Word of God is packed with demonstrations and illustrations of God's faithfulness towards mankind. He cannot lie! Whatever He says, He will do. Rest assured He will do it to completion, even against all odds.

God delivered the Children of Israel from oppression, cruelty, and bondage in Egypt. The journey to the Promised Land was supposed to be a short one (some scholars say 11 days), but instead it took 40 years!

The Israelites vacillated between obeying God and rebelling against God, succumbing at times to their own passions and lusts. Hence, to their detriment, the journey detoured 40 long years in the Wilderness.

Nevertheless, the faithfulness of God remained true. Despite their human frailties and weaknesses, God never forsook them nor gave up on them. As their Emmanuel, He brought them into the Good Land against all odds. (See Joshua 21: 43 -45).

The same is true today!

In our generation, God is still working faithfully. Despite our failures, the chaos in the world, the hopelessness we may feel at times, the pain and regrets of life, let's not forget to encourage one another and lean steadfastly on the Word of God. He is not a man that He should lie (Numbers 23:19). He can be trusted above all to bring us through to a good end!

Prayer

Our Father, we thank and praise You. Your NAME shall always be in our mouth, faithful and true, everlasting friend and ally.

Sonia Brown

BIBLICAL HEROES

What is That in Thine Hand?

"And the Lord said unto him, 'What is that in thine hand?' And he said, 'A rod.'"

--Exodus 4:2

For Moses, it might have been a shepherd's staff seeing he was a shepherd taking care of his father-in-law's sheep. This same question is being posed to you today, "What do you have in your hand?" The Lord wants to use whatever He has equipped you with to bring glory to His name. First, we must make it available for His use. In essence, "Cast it on the ground."

The rod was vital to his work as a shepherd, yet the Lord said, "Throw it down." God had another purpose for it. Throw it down!! God had a job that needed to be done and He needed a worker. Moses didn't see himself as being qualified for the task, so God asked, "What is in thine hand?" In his hand was a rod that had been used to lead the children of Israel in the wilderness. In essence, it was tried and proven.

> Are there things that we are holding on to that we need to cast to the ground?

When we give up what is important to us, the Lord will tell us when to pick it up again. Many of us have hidden talents or undiscovered gifts that God wants to use. Even though the task might seem impossible, God can use it; we have no excuse. Ordinary things can become extraordinary to accomplish God's plan.

Are you willing to turn over your rod to become the instrument for God to use? Are you using what's in your hand for God's glory? Are you using your position, talents, and gifts to bring others into His kingdom? James reminds us that, "Every good gift is from above and cometh down from the Father of lights" (1: 7).

God has entrusted to each of us talents that are to be used for His glory.

Prayer

Father, help me to be obedient to your call and to use what has been given to me. Help me to become more conscious of your gifts and use them for your glory. Amen.

Beverly Coker

Joseph's Coat of Many Colors

"and he made him a coat of many colors."

--Genesis 37: 3

All of us know how special we feel when we are given something that is beautiful and unique. It is especially more meaningful when it's a gift from someone whom we cherish. Joseph's father loved him and gave him this special gift. It exemplifies to me God's love for us. Paul reminds us that "For by grace you have been saved..." (Ephesians 2:8-9).

As much as Joseph loved his coat and wore it with pride, in a moment when faced with temptation, he was willing to let it go and leave it behind. At that time when the King's wife came after him, he was not concerned about looking pretty or losing something of value, but he left his coat in her hand and fled (See Genesis 39:12). This was not the same coat he was wearing. His brothers dipped that one in blood to prove to Jacob that Joseph was dead (See Genesis 37:32-33). (Gen. 39:12). How many of us would be wavering about our decision and looking back to see if we could retrieve it? Paul says, "Forgetting those things which are behind, ...I press..." (Philippians 3: 13-14). Little did Joseph know that by giving up his coat he was gaining a far greater gift, a throne. Through this test, God was preparing him for his destiny to reign. Whatever you might be going through today, it's in preparing for a greater assignment. God is testing to see if you will overcome in a moment of temptation.

The Lord has something great for us, but you must go through something to overcome. The Bible tells us, "And the Lord was with Joseph" (See Genesis 39: 2). He is with you. Don't give up. There is better ahead.

Prayer

Lord, help us not to yield to temptation but to seek your help in being an overcomer. Remind us that you have greatness in store for us if we trust you and persevere. Amen.

Beverly Coker.

A Man Called Job

"The Lord gave; and the Lord hath taken away; blessed be the name of the Lord"

--Job 1:20

Although I have not studied the life of Job extensively, today I would like to focus my attention on this man whom the Bible states "was the greatest of all the men of the east" (v.3). He was "perfect and upright" (v.1.1). How many of us could be considered perfect and upright? Job was such a godly man that he became the subject of a debate in Heaven.

There are lessons we can learn from this man, lessons that are as relevant today as they were then.

> Why do the righteous suffer? Why do bad things happen to good people?

None of us could withstand the pain and suffering that Job experienced, yet "In all this, Job sinned not nor charged God foolishly" (v.1:20-22). He lost his possessions, his family, his health, but he did not lose his faith. In fact, the Bible tells us that "he shaved his head, and fell down upon the ground and worshipped." Not many of us could worship when we have been stripped of everything that is meaningful to us. We must remember that whatever we have, the Lord gave it to us, and he can take it away if He wishes.

Job must have questioned God at some point of his life. He endured intense pain, and pain often brings us to a place of brokenness. He found himself in very challenging situations. Tragedy struck when he was at the pinnacle of success. How could this happen to a man who feared

God? Yet, Job did not complain, because when he reflected on his yesterdays, he realized how blessed he had been.

"Though you slay me, yet will I trust you."

Most of us are fair-weather Christians, but the true condition of our heart is revealed when we are exposed to suffering.

The Book of Job raises the issue of why Christians suffer. Job teaches us such valuable lessons, as trouble is the common denominator of mankind. He exercised patience to get him through this period of his life. James writes, "ye have heard of the patience of Job" (James 5:11).

Can you endure such calamity and not curse God? Let's see!!

Prayer

Our Gracious God, help us to learn the lessons of your servant Job, who reminded us that You will never leave us nor forsake us. Amen.

Beverly Coker

God's Choice Servant

"I have found David, the son of Jesse, a man after mine own heart...."

--Acts 13:22 *KJV*

David was just a young man in his teens when God called him to be King. He was only a shepherd, but God had great plans for his life. David had great potential, even though the people around him did not recognize his worth.

Like all of us, David had many liabilities that could have prevented him from becoming King. His family, for one, was dysfunctional. In today's society, we would have convened a committee to depose him from his Kingship. But God protected His servant and subsequently brought good out of evil. God can take every experience, turn it around, and make it work for your good.

David's life revealed his human qualities. He had his moments of triumphs and his setbacks. He was constantly under attack, even living in caves to escape from his enemies. But God preserved him because He had a plan for his life.

"Being confident of this very thing, that he which hath began a good work in you will perform it until the day of Jesus Christ" (Phil. 1:6).

When we recall the beautiful Psalms that David wrote, we realize that he had to have gone through much in order to provide such great encouragement. In Psalm 51, when he asked for forgiveness after his adulterous relationship, he was being transparent in letting us know that we too serve a forgiving God.

Success comes with challenges and you will soon find that not everyone celebrates your success.

"When the Philistines heard that they had anointed David King over Israel they went up in search of David" (I Sam. 5:17).

They wanted to kill him, but again, God protected him. Success doesn't come easy. You have to fight for it and fight to keep it. That's why you need God's anointing and guidance if you are to survive your storm.

David was described as a man after God's own heart. David demonstrated a heart of forgiveness, knowing that he had been forgiven by God. After he became King, he inquired if there was anyone left of the household of Saul that he could show kindness to them. He was pointed to Methshiboseth, the grandson of Saul who was crippled. When David found this young man, he made him sit at his table for the rest of his life. What forgiveness! Knowing what Saul, his grandfather had done.

Indeed, David was a choice servant because he exhibited Christlike qualities, one of which was the power to forgive.

Prayer

Lord, I ask that you give me a forgiving spirit. Amen.

Beverly Coker

Uniting to Move Forward

"Entreat me not to leave thee, or to return from following after thee. For whither thou goest, I will go; and where thou lodgest, I will lodge: thy people shall be my people, and thy God my God."

--Ruth 1:16

In 1999, I had the privilege of sitting at the feet of a dear Christian woman, Mother Kathleen Beckford-Davids, as she preached on the topic "Uniting to Move Forward." She has since gone to be with the Lord, but as I reflect on this sermon, I wanted to include it in this Devotional as a tribute to her.

Mother Davids reminded us that Naomi continued to move forward despite the adverse circumstances in her life. She had lost her husband and two sons, but she never lost her faith. She trusted in a God who promised not to leave us nor forsake us. Like many of us, Naomi suffered greatly. However, she did not allow her sufferings and grief to impede her progress. Again, we are reminded that regardless of the calamities and burdens we sometimes experience, we can still move forward.

Naomi was blessed and highly favored, not with money but with the quality of love that she enjoyed with her daughters-in-law. Love conquers grief, empowers and gives us the ability to move forward together.

Naomi encountered a crossroad when she was forced to make a life changing decision. Her decision was to return to her homeland of Judah though broken and grieved. One of her daughters-in-law chose to go with her, the other returned home to her people. How could she? Before we become judgmental, let us reflect on the choices we make every day in our lives. Mother Davids reminded us that sometimes we lose sight of what we should do, but in those circumstances, our best approach should be to wait on the Lord.

Ruth stayed with her mother-in-law; the rest is history. She is noted as the ancestor of Jesus Christ. The Bible tells us that Ruth produced Obed, the father of Jesse, the father of David (See Ruth 4:21,22). Finally, Jesus came from the offspring of David. When we face our bitter times, we are reminded that God welcomes our honest prayers.

Prayer

Heavenly Father, we thank You that even when we face situations beyond our control, You are there with us. You always have a plan to work in our favor. Although we cannot see the outcome, You have designed a path for us. For that we say, "Thank you." Amen.

Beverly Coker/ Mother Davids

Made to Forget

"God has made me forget all my troubles."

--Genesis 41:51

As I write this devotional, it's almost the end of the year, a time of reflection and taking stock of our lives. For many, it was a year of hardship, bitterness, and pain. Do you realize how much easier it is to remember the pain than the glory? Let 's think of a few individuals who had all reasons to be bitter…" but God."

Joseph was deeply wounded by his brothers who sold him to strangers. In a strange land, he was imprisoned for a crime he did not commit. Joseph had all rights to become bitter, but he realized that it's not what they did to him, but how he responded that determined the outcome.

God had a plan for Joseph, and in order to fulfill God's plan, he had to release his resentment and let it go. He refused to see himself as a victim. That is why he was able to say, "God had made me forget all my troubles." Joseph turned his situation into a positive endeavor to become a blessing to those who had hurt him.

Paul, prior to his encounter with God was in essence, a terrorist. He persecuted the church and watched as Stephen was being stoned to death. He was a menace to the early church…"But God." We might wonder, how could the church forgive such a person and how could he forgive himself? He admitted in Galatians 1:13: "…how that beyond measure I persecuted the church of God, and wasted it." Paul did not deny his actions; he faced his wrongdoing, confessed them to God, who alone had the power to forgive. Paul confessed in Romans 7:24, "O wretched man that I am! who shall deliver me from the body of this death?" Paul found grace through the power of forgiveness by which he was able to forgive himself and wrote almost one third of the New Testament.

"Forgetting those things which are behind ...I press toward the mark for the prize" (Philippians 3:13).

The greatest example of forgiveness was Jesus. He experienced excruciating pain on the cross by the hands of his enemies. His disciples betrayed him, forsook him and denied him. Yet, his statement from the cross, "Lord forgive them for they know not what they do." This applied not only to the thief who was being crucified with him, but to his disciples and in particular to you and me. If Joseph, Paul, and Jesus could exemplify forgiveness through their action, then you and I need to do the same.

Prayer

Father, thank you for allowing us to move beyond the past to a life set free through the power of forgiveness. Amen.

Beverly Coker

SPIRITUAL GROWTH AND MATURITY

Keep on Pressing

"I press toward the mark for the prize of the high calling of God in Christ Jesus."

--Philippians 3: 14

Each of us is engaged in the race of life. We enter the race at birth and continue until death. However, Paul had a different type of race in mind when he penned this verse. Since his conversion, he found himself running in a race with Heaven as his goal. He realized that in a race one could easily become distracted and weighed down with situations from the past. In order to get to the finish, Paul was resolved to forget about the past and press towards what was ahead. What was there in his past that could have created a distraction for him?

There was a dark side to this brilliant personality. He persecuted Christians, and in fact, was on his way to Damascus to carry out his evil acts when he saw the light. Paul was present when Stephen was being martyred, though he did not actively participate. He held the clothes of those who stoned Stephen to death.

These and perhaps other memories from the past could have haunted him. Nevertheless, he had reached a point in his Christian race when he wanted to forget those things and focus on matters of eternal value. In order to get to the finish line, he had to strain toward what was ahead. He could not take this race for granted.

How much discipline do you cultivate in your life to make it to the finish? How much time do you spend reading the Word of God and talking to your Father, the One who will give the prize at the end of the race? Paul realized the importance of engaging in these spiritual activities so "one thing I do….I press" (Philippians 1: 13).

In this race, people do fall, but they get up and continue in the race. Proverbs 24:16 "For a just man falleth seven times, and riseth up again." Failure isn't final. You can rise again. Failure is allowing yourself to stay down when the Bible proclaims, "I can do all things through Christ which strengthens me" (Philippians 4: 13). Paul did not see himself as being perfect, so he disciplined himself in order to stay in the race. "Lest that by any means, when I have preached to others, I myself should be a castaway." (2 Corinthians 9:27). Stay in the race!

Prayer:

Lord, at times I grow weary and want to give up, but those are times when I feel your arms around me lifting me back in the race. Thank you for being my strength. Amen.

Beverly Coker

He Knows Me

"I want to know Christ and the power of his resurrection and the fellowship of sharing in his suffering becoming like him in His death."

--Philippians 3:10 *NIV*

When we become one with Christ Jesus by trusting in Him, we experience the power that raised Him from the dead. That same power will help us to live a victorious life as we are daily renewed by His power and presence. What an awful death He suffered just for you and me. But as His life was predestined for the cross of Calvary so are our lives predestined to serve our God. May we be empowered by the resurrected Jesus. We can count on our God that He is able to take care of us.

We will not be defeated by the deceptions and the onslaught of the enemy because God has everything in His control. The way may be rocky and steep, but as we travel along, His hand will guide us. Sing a song of praise, cry if you may, but be encouraged that our God is an on-time God. Troubles will not last; difficulties will not last because God has a purpose for your life and mine. We raise the banner of hope in God today because He's watching us from a distance.

The song says, "He touch me, oh He touch me, and oh the joy that floods my soul. Something happened and now I know, He touched me and made me whole." Wholeness means that God completes everything in your life and nothing is lacking. Things may seem dark but there is always hope beyond darkness. There is always daylight after midnight and so our hope is in an unfailing God because He knows more that we know ourselves. Praise

His name.

Prayer

Lord, my heart longs for you. My desire is towards you. I seek your face because I know that my help cometh from the Lord the maker of heaven and earth. Help me daily that I will get close to you in a remarkable way. Therefore, upon the confidence of your word I take courage in trusting you daily as I serve you with my whole heart. I wait on you Lord, in Jesus name. Amen.

Coleene Shaw

Knowing God

"That I may know Him and the power of His resurrection."

--Philippians 3:10

Let us look at the benefits of knowing God and the differences between knowing God and knowing about him (Job 22:21). Many people know about Him but do not really know Him in a personal manner. It is not enough for us to know Him in theory but not in practice. When we experience God through His grace and mercy, we come to know Him. The more He blesses us, the more we hear Him speaking to us, the more we shall know Him.

It should be the desire of every Christian to know God in a deeper more intimate way. With the challenges of this life, a surface relationship cannot suffice. We must seek deeper meaning through daily communication which is prayer and reading of His Word.

Paul had an encounter with God through which he eventually came to know Him as a friend, healer, and protector, but Paul was not satisfied with that level of intimacy. Paul wanted to know the power of His resurrection and fellowship of His suffering (Philippians 3:10). Through what power was He resurrected and what made Him endure the suffering? That's why we need to seek to know Him better, so we may experience a greater understanding of the power of the cross.

In today's world where we become so busy and caught up with the mundane things of this life, it's hard to find time to know God. It takes effort and a diligent desire to know Him. As we spend time to get to know our friends and especially our intimate partners, so we should spend time to get to know God. He is more important than these individuals, yet we spend so little time talking with Him and spending time in His presence. There are many benefits to a deeper more meaningful relationship with God. I challenge you to try it and see for yourself.

Prayer

Father, teach me to know you in a way that I have not known you before. I seek for a deeper relationship with you. In Jesus' name. Amen.

Beverly Coker

Growing in Christ: Part I

"That the God of our Lord Jesus Christ, the Father of glory, may give unto you the spirit of wisdom and revelation in the knowledge of him."

--Ephesians 1:17

Some time ago, I heard this story: "A female member of a Catholic church went to confession. She confessed to the priest that she had gone on a date and in a moment of passion had sinned. The priest prayed with her and instructed her to say, "Three Holy Mary," To the priest's surprise she said, "Six Holy Mary." When asked by the priest why she said six, she replied that it might happen again.

When we come to God by accepting, acknowledging, and being sold out to Jesus as Savior and Lord, we receive the infilling of the Spirit of God. It is by salvation through Jesus by the grace of God. It is not by our works. We go through water baptism to announce to the world that we have been bought with a price (the precious blood of Jesus). Water baptism does not save us, just as our works do not save us. However, as James 2:26 says, the body without the spirit is dead, so faith without works is dead also.

We who are not Catholics are not required to go to a priest to confess. However, we must confess our sins to God and continue our spiritual growth. It cannot be done without the blessed Holy Spirit working in us to give the Spirit of wisdom and discernment. The spirit of wisdom and discernment allows us to grow in Christ and know Him better. It is a journey filled with experiences, but the ultimate goal is for a lasting and increasing relationship with Jesus Christ and the hope to which He has called us. (Eph. 1: 18, 19).

Prayer

Father God, I ask for your guidance through the blessed Holy Spirit to increase in knowledge about you. Amen.

JAT

Growing in Christ: Part II

"Wherefore, my beloved, as ye have always obeyed, not as in my presence only, but now much more in my absence, work out your own salvation with fear and trembling."

--Philippians 2: 12

The entire epistle of Paul to the Philippians may be summarized as a charge or encouragement to them for faithfulness in "growth in Christ". Specifically, in Philippians 2: 12 reminds them and by extension all of us of our responsibilities in "growing in Christ."

Having a fear of God should not be interpreted as being afraid of God. God wants us to be in fellowship with Him and to be afraid of Him would not strengthen this fellowship. Fearing God is accepting that He is God and that He must be held in reverence. His path to everlasting life is fixed. We must honor Him and follow that path which is salvation through His Son Jesus Christ. Proverbs 1:7 says "the fear of the Lord is the beginning of knowledge." We cannot begin to attain knowledge of Him unless we first respect and honor Him.

Our Praise and Worship is one way of honoring Him. Growing in Christ is an overall way to honor Him. Working out our own salvation reminds us that it is about our individual relationship with Him. No pastor or priest or relative can do that for us. They can teach and exhort under the leading of the Holy Spirit and shepherd us towards a Christ-like like, but ultimately it is our yielding to the Holy Spirit that brings spiritual growth.

We always remain in awe and the feeling in our hearts is literally a trembling with excitement and hope.

Prayer

Father God, I thank you for your patience with me as I seek to be more Christ-like under the urging of your Blessed Holy Spirit. Amen.

JAT

Managing Life's Transitions: Part I

"And the sons of the prophets said unto Elisha, Behold now, the place where we dwell with thee is too strait for us. Let us go, we pray thee, unto Jordan, and take thence every man a beam, and let us make us a place there, where we may dwell. And he answered, Go ye. And one said, Be content, I pray thee, and go with thy servants. And he answered, I will go. So he went with them. And when they came to Jordan, they cut down wood. But as one was felling a beam, the axe head fell into the water: and he cried, and said, Alas, master! for it was borrowed. And the man of God said, Where fell it? And he shewed him the place. And he cut down a stick, and cast it in thither; and the iron did swim. Therefore, said he, Take it up to thee. And he put out his hand, and took it."

--2 Kings 6:1-7

Our journey through life can be challenging yet exciting when God goes with us. Transitions create new boundaries (geographical, relational, emotional and financial) which challenge us to grow as we adapt to our new environment. The Scripture reference above, gives an account of some principles which should help us understand and navigate transitions more easily.

Elisha's protégées recognized that it was time to move; where they were had become "too small" (verse 1 NKJV). The original Hebrew suggests the place was physically narrow and that they were also facing distressing, adversarial circumstances.

> *Transitions require an understanding of our season and an alertness to shift at the right time (Gal.4:4).*

Lack of vision and insensitivity to the voice of the Spirit can confine us to the wrong season and cause us to contend with problems God never intended for us (Num. 14:42-45). Elisha's servants valued his presence and invited him to accompany them (vs. 3-4).

> *Transitions involve defining the boundaries of relationships through alignments and separations.*

Fellowship with God should be the most important relationship in every form and phase of transitioning.

The axe head which represents a life of substance (character, security, livelihood, relationships, health etc.), was suddenly lost (v 5).

> *Sudden and disheartening transitions can leave us feeling uncertain and helpless.*

The Master is always there to help (Ps. 46:1). A stick, symbolizing the cross of Jesus Christ, was thrown in the water causing the axe head to float (vs. 6-7). The power of the cross of Jesus Christ transcends time, restores losses, and enables us to continue building when life falls apart.

The servant was able to recall where he lost the axe head and retrieve it (vs.6-7).

> *Memorialize transitions with landmarks (Prov. 22:28).*

Landmarks are memorials and testimonies of significant experiences which strengthen our relationship with the Lord. They are reminders of where we made resolutions with problems in our past. Landmarks have personal and generational implications and give us the faith to overcome future barriers (Rev. 12:11). Unless God, our Creator, is involved in all aspects of life's transitions, our journey is futile. *(Ps. 127:1).*

Prayer

Lord Jesus, I submit to You as You guide me through every facet of life by Your divine wisdom. Amen.

Sherill Thomas

Managing Life's Transitions Part II: Dying to Self

"I have been crucified with Christ; it is no longer I who live, but Christ lives in me."

--Gal. 2:20

Transitional experiences are meaningless if we do not emerge on the other side with some awareness of personal growth and maturity. Transitions serve as pathways to our future and preparation for our purpose. A major characteristic of the transitional process is that of dying to one's self. The "new creature" (2 Cor. 5:17) who is now living that new and abundant life in Jesus Christ, becomes evident only when the "old man" (Eph. 4:22) has died. Jesus affirmed this truth in John 12:24: a grain of wheat becomes fruitful only after it has died.

In 2 Kings 6:2, Elisha and his servants transitioned to Jordan, a name which symbolizes death. While there, the axe head, which was instrumental for building a new life, was lost in the water then retrieved, a process symbolic of death and resurrection. Moses died while leading the Israelites in their transition from Egypt to the Promised Land. To fully transition into their new identity as children of God and inheritors of His promises, the people were instructed by God to "go over this Jordan" (Josh. 1:2). The self-absorbed, self-pleasing wilderness mentality, characterized by complaining, rebelling against God, and idolatrous worship has to die in order to make room for the resurrected Christ.

Hallmarks of a dead or dying self include:

- *Not being easily offended.* (Prov. 18:19).

- *Not always defending ourselves; not always trying to prove we are right even if we are; not bent on having the last say whenever there is an argument* (Mark 15:1-5).
- *Putting the needs of others above our own without compromising God's standard (1 Cor. 8:9-13).*

The crucifixion of the self is an ongoing, redemptive process. Our daily choices are true indicators of how much the "old man" has died and subsequently, how much Christ is alive in us (Rom. 6:1-6). The power to live a triumphant and impacting Christian life resides in us in the form of the Holy Spirit. Death, in any form, which makes room for Christ to live, is always gain. (Philippians 1:21).

Prayer:

Holy Spirit, thank you for showing me areas of my life in which I have not died to self. With your help, I chose to make choices that will consistently reflect the resurrected Christ in me and influence others to serve Him. Amen.

Sherill Thomas

The Power of the Tongue: Part I

"Even so the tongue is a little member, and boasteth great things. Behold, how great a matter a little fire kindleth."

--(James 3: 5

Growing up, I heard the following adage repeatedly: "There are three things you can't take back:

> (1) a spent arrow (2) a spoken word and (3) a lost opportunity."

In the selected scripture from James, we are warned that as Christians, we ought to try to control our tongue. Though small a member relative to the other parts of the body, the tongue is a mighty tool. James likens it to:

1. The helm of a ship that is able to steer and control the ship in the fiercest storm (verse 4).
2. A small flame that can develop into a fire burning out thousands of acres of forest (verse 5).
3. A bit in a horse's mouth that can control the entire movement of the horse (verse 3).

As Christians, we should endeavor to use speech to be positive (Proverbs 6:2 and Proverbs 4: 20). We can bring the good news of the gospel to a sinful world. We can take care to make our utterances gracious, bringing hope, peace, and joy to troubled minds as Jesus did (Luke 4: 22). For new Christians, the mouth can be used to praise God and make confession as they accept salvation through Jesus Christ.

Recently in the United States, a young lady was charged with aiding and abetting her boyfriend's suicide by the language she used in emails to him. The tongue can bless or curse (v. 10), but as Christians, we ought to use it to bless. By ourselves, it is impossible to speak positive words at all times, but the Blessed Holy Spirit will help us.

Prayer

Father God, I pray that the utterances I make may be guided by the Holy Spirit and will always seek to glorify You. Amen.

JAT

The Power of the Tongue: Part II

"For in many things we offend all. If any man offend not in word, the same is a perfect man, and able also to bridle the whole body."

-- James 3: 2

The second adage that I heard often was, "If you cannot speak good of anyone or add positive words to a situation, keep your tongue."

It would seem that this scripture and the above adage could cause us to err on the side of caution and say little; however, holding our tongue in certain situations when we should speak up can be as bad as speaking evil. Very often, false doctrine about Christianity is being uttered and we know it is not true and we remain silent.

People's faith comes by hearing the Word of God, so one of the reasons we should study the Word of God is to be able to correct false doctrines. Sometimes, untrue and unkind things are being said about persons and we know they are not true. We remain silent and this might be assumed to indicate agreement. The problem may be that we find it difficult to find the words to rebuke with compassion.

Ephesians 4: 14-15 teaches that we should speak the truth in love as we grow in Christ so we can promote unity. By ourselves it is impossible, but with guidance of the Holy Spirit, we can.

Prayer

Lord, give me boldness and understanding through the Holy Spirit so that I can defend the gospel and offer correction with love and humility. Amen.

JAT

Being in God's Presence

"In Thy Presence is fulness of Joy."

--Psalm 16: 11 *NJV*

One morning, I received a call from a friend requesting that I come over to see her. I did not ask why; I just knew that I needed to visit my friend. She told me that she had another appointment and suggested that I come within a certain time frame. I hurriedly left my home to get to her during the suggested time. On my way, it suddenly occurred to me that I had forgotten my cell phone. Knowing the importance of having a phone with me at all times, I felt like returning home to retrieve my phone, but decided against that idea.

I arrived at my friend's home and realized that she was not there. What am I going to do with my time with no phone to return calls? It somehow dawned on me that right there in my car, I could spend time alone in the presence of the Lord. There would be no distractions nor interruptions. This, then, became a blessed time as I basked in the presence of God.

Psalm 95: 2 reminds us to come before His presence with thanksgiving. I offered thanksgiving for everything. As I counted my blessings, I found more things to give thanks for. Waiting for my friend, I became increasingly aware of the presence of God. No wonder David said, "If I ascend up into Heaven, thou art there. If I make my bed in hell, behold thou art there. If I take the wings of the morning and dwell in the uttermost parts of the sea; even there shall thy hand lead me, and the right hand shall hold me" (Psalm 139: 8-10).

During the time of waiting, no one knew where I was. I could not be tracked, which gave me a very peaceful feeling. No wonder we are told to "be still and know that I am God."

> In order to overcome the busyness of this life, we need to wait upon the Lord to get our strength renewed.

As I waited, I began to discern that the delay was my appointment with God. I could identify with Jacob in Genesis 28:16 when he said, "Surely, the Lord is in this place and I knew it not." It is good to know that we can never get away from His presence, even when we try to escape the cares of this life. Thank God for His promise that gives us the assurance that He will always be with us! Indeed, it gives us "fullness of joy."

Prayer

Father, thank you for your presence in my life. Even when I lose sight of you in times of brokenness, loneliness, and despair, You always find ways of reminding me that I am yours. Amen.

Beverly Coker

Continue to Bear Fruit

"They shall still bring forth fruit in old age."

--Psalm 92:14

Life offers to us many seasons. Ecclesiastes 3:2 reminds us, "A time to be born, and a time to die." Shakespeare describes it in terms of stages.: "All the world's a stage, and all the men and women merely players; they have their exits and entrances; and one man in his time plays many parts." If we are blessed to make it to the end stage, there is still something beautiful about life. Most of us wish to live to see the winter season. Winter is when you can count your accomplishments, enjoy your retirement, and celebrate life.

On a regular basis, I visit the homes of elderly saints who are no longer able to join the fellowship at church. I sometimes remind them of the days when they were young, vibrant, and active in the work of the Lord. In a moment of forgetfulness, some need to be reminded that the seed they planted then are flourishing today and bearing fruits in the lives of another generation. They need to be reminded that "gray hair is a crown of splendor" (Proverbs 16:31). Their lives can still influence those who visit them. They can minister and pray with others on the telephone.

With the winter or golden age comes wisdom, and wisdom is often in short supply.

Yes, this generation has more knowledge, but are they using that knowledge wisely?

Let us encourage young people to treat the seniors with respect and gratitude for the values they have instilled in us and the work they did for the Kingdom of God. Remind the elders that "life is not over until it's over," therefore, they still have much to contribute in terms of the way they face the winter years. They can be an example of grace, wisdom, courage, and an unending desire to worship God. Paul says, he fought a good fight, kept the faith and finished the course (See 1 Timothy 4:7).

The Bible gives us examples of individuals whose later end was greater than their beginning (Job 42:12). Moses was 120 years old when he died, and his eyes were not dim, nor his natural face abated (Deuteronomy 37:7). Forgetting those things which are behind, let each senior endeavor to obtain the joy that lies ahead- "The lines have fallen unto me…I have a goodly heritage" (Psalm 16:6).

Prayer

Thank you for the years of your faithfulness to me. Help me not to look back with regret but with hope in You. Amen.

Beverly Coker

Equipping Ourselves with the Word of God

"Study to shew thyself approved unto God, a workman that needeth not to be ashamed, rightly dividing the word of truth."

--2 Timothy 2:15

In our Christian walk, we all want to get God's approval in all our endeavors. This certainly is not an easy task but "All things are possible if we only believe" (Mark 9:23). Knowing the mind of Christ will channel us in the right direction. How is this accomplished? By equipping ourselves with the Word of God. This means spending quality time studying His Word. His Word is like a tool. The more you use it, the easier it becomes to understand.

Paul instructs Timothy to make diligent and effective use of the scriptures in order to live holy and righteous (See 2 Timothy 2:15). God knows what is best for us, so he has given His Word which is His blueprint for us to live Godly lives. His Word is true. When we know the Truth, we don't have to be ashamed.

God knows our capabilities. He created us for His purpose. He is the Potter and we are the clay. He craves our obedience in studying His Word. Romans 10:17 says, "Faith cometh by hearing and hearing by the Word of God." We cannot divorce ourselves from the Word of God because it is through the Word of God that our faith grows.

Prayer

Lord, please help us to study Your Word and hide it in our hearts so we will not sin against Thee. Amen.

Rev. Mildred Shaw/G.A.T.

Transforming Power

"Therefore, if any man be in Christ, he is a new creature, old things are passed away, behold all things are become new."

--2 Corinthians 5:17

Today, as I drove by this particular house, it occurred to me that its transformation is ideal for my devotional. I have lived in this neighborhood for several years. For as long as I can recall, this house has been run-down, dilapidated, and an eye-sore to the neighborhood. Families have even relocated because of its closeness to their homes. No one wants to be associated with an image that conjures up failure and hopelessness.

The story is told that after the death of his wife, this gentleman's life took a downward spiral. This was reflected in the manner in which he kept his house and yard. This winter, we observed dump trucks parked in front of the house. Vans with maintenance workers went steadily in and out, even a Porta Potty was parked on the front lawn. We knew something was about to happen. Before long, the house was torn apart, large pieces of furniture were dumped, and reconstruction began.

Today, as I drove by, I paused to admire this beautiful white house with gorgeous black shutters replacing the image of the old house. One could never imagine the transformation. It's now a pleasure to be in this neighborhood. It makes me wonder if the neighbors who had moved out, are now regretting their decision.

The house reminds me of the transforming power of Jesus Christ. He takes our old sinful nature and replaces it with new goals, values, attitude, and a new life. When we accept Christ, our lives are changed for the better. People should not see the old house in which we once lived, but the new house that reflects God's beauty. God's work begins on the inside, then becomes noticeable on the outside. The change in the human nature is only possible through faith in Jesus Christ.

Yes, if any man be in Christ, the junk that we once harbored on the inside will be removed and the Fruit of the Spirit will emanate from our existence. People should want to associate with us when our lives have been transformed.

Prayer

Father God, thank you for the transforming power that you offer to each of us. Daily, you prove to us that we cannot be the same once you have taken residence in our heart. Amen.

Beverly Coker

Wash Me Over Again

"Create in me a clean heart, oh God, and renew a right spirit within me."

--Psalm 51:10

Let's look at two words that this Psalm implies:

> **Sanctify:** Cleanse, set apart for special use, make holy
>
> **Consecrate:** To separate, to set apart for sacred purposes.

These words are interchangeable.

We must search ourselves daily and measure ourselves against the Word, so that Jesus can cleanse us and renew a right spirt within us. As someone once said, "No one knows oneself as one's own self."

In John 17:17, Jesus said to his Father, "Sanctify them through thy Truth, thy Word is Truth!"

As we partake daily in the breaking of the bread of the Word, Jesus is actually consecrating us through His word. Psalm 51 was chosen by the Holy Spirit to move us unto higher spiritual ground. The more of the Word we partake of each day, the more like Jesus we become. The more consecrated our temples are, we become better vessels fitted for the Master's use. Remember, we are still on the Potter's wheel.

Another aspect of being consecrated is the place of humility in our lives. If we are not humble before the Lord, we will not be able to hear what he is saying to us about ourselves. Consecration or Sanctification is not just for a day or a week, but an ongoing process. So, let us not get weary in our efforts to become more consecrated, but let us endeavor to strive for the Mastery. As an encouragement to us, Jesus will see us through, because He is our strength, strength like no other, and He promised never to leave us nor forsake us. (See Hebrews 13:5). Amen.

Prayer:

Father God, create in each of us a rightful spirit. Help us to present ourselves to You daily for renewed consecration. Amen.

Paulette Joseph

It's Turnaround Time

"For I know the thoughts that I think toward you, saith the Lord, thoughts of peace and not of evil, to give you an expected end."

-- Jeremiah 29: 11

I am writing this devotion just after the New Year. This is usually a time of reflection, a time to examine our lives and a time to take stock of the past year. As we look back, we tend to maximize our shortcomings, minimize our strength and often regret things said, done, or not done. Sometimes, as Christians, we can go through periods of introspection, resulting in feelings of depression, knowing that we did not accomplish God's plan for our lives. However, these feelings should not immobilize us as we enter a new year, or a new season. Regardless of our shortcomings of the past year, God is able to turn it around. In other words, let the past be the past. God has new plans for you this year. *"I know the plans I have for you, saith the Lord."* He is able to take your brokenness and make them whole again.

There is an element of uncertainty to each new day, but we enter the future with confidence that the Lord promises to be with us. *"He will never leave you nor forsake you."* As you embark on a new beginning, think optimistically about where you are going and the great possibilities that lie ahead. Visualize every challenge as an opportunity for growth.

This year, look beyond the failures of the past and realize that God can use those situations to teach us valuable lessons, lessons that could launch you into what lies ahead. Let us not dwell on the mistakes of the past but embrace this new opportunity to make right. Remove the veil of unbelief, fear, and low self-confidence as you move towards a life of abundance. God's plans for you will cause you to prosper, restore hope, and give you an expected end.

Has God intervened and turned your circumstances around in the past? He is still a "turn around God" so expect great things from Him this year.

Prayer

Lord, I commit my future to you knowing that you will not leave me nor forsake me. Please work out your plan and purpose for my life. Amen.

Beverly Coker

Are You a Potted Oak?

"He shall be like a tree planted ... whatever he does shall prosper."

--Psalm 1:3

Greatness is in you! An oak is a symbol of strength and endurance and it cannot grow to its full potential if potted. The root system must be unencumbered to be properly nourished to sustain the height (possibly 65 to 100 feet) and far reaching breadth.

You may have been planted in the wrong environment because of extenuating circumstances: fear of failure, missed or lack of opportunities, misfortune in life, or maybe someone said you'd never succeed. Now you're stuck . . . in a flower pot! The good news is, you can be transplanted – starting today.

The angel didn't speak to Gideon about his present condition; he spoke to what was buried on the inside – ***"a mighty man of valor, a deliverer"*** (Judges 6:12). Moses tried bargaining with God to send someone else to Pharaoh (See Exodus. 4:10-15). The prodigal son made poor choices, but he returned home (See Luke 15:20-24).

God sees you struggling to survive in that "pot." Let Him transplant you so the "oak" in you can thrive. He takes pleasure in your prosperity (See Psalm 35:2). Decide that you want a change in your circumstances. Be specific and set realistic goals about what you want changed. Ask God for strategies. The Holy Spirit will guide you and send assistance through the right people (See Jeremiah. 29:11). Be willing to stay the course. Roots take time to adjust to new environments and so will you. Break the pot! ". . . He shall grow like a cedar in Lebanon" (Psalm 92:12).

Prayer

Father, thank you for perfecting that which concerns me; for the faith, strength and patience it takes to change, in Jesus' Name, Amen.

Monica Case Williams

Be Still

"Be still and know that I am God. I will be exhalted among the heathen. I will be exhalted in the earth. The Lord of hosts is with us. The God of Jacob is our refuge."

--Psalm 45:10-11

Life can become challenging at times. We find ourselves frustrated and trying, in our own effort, to fix the situations that we are in. We can be so caught up that we find ourselves focusing on the frustration and becoming distracted from moving into our purpose.

There are times when we become impatient with the process because the process is not always to our liking. Things do not seem to be moving as quickly or in the direction that we had anticipated that they would move. We find ourselves in the flesh trying to concoct our own remedies for our problems. There are times that we have to move out and do something, and there are times when we are admonished to be still.

The stillness that God is talking about is not just a lack of action, but it is more of a resting in the promises of God. Sometimes our efforts seem fruitless because it seems as if we are moving on a tread mill - expending a lot of energy but making no progress. Walking but not going anywhere.

We can be still because we are resting in the promises of God. We can be still because we serve a God with a proven track record of victory. We can be still because when we are still, God will, without fail, move on our behalf.

Prayer

Heavenly Father, teach us to be still in Your presence.

Teach us to wait upon You. In You there is hope and victory.

Rev. Laverne Ramsey

What's Your Worth?

"Not redeemed with corruptible things . . . but with the precious blood of Jesus Christ."

--1 Peter 1:18-19

No, not your net worth. What's your value? You were bought with the ***priceless*** blood of God's Son, Jesus Christ! You owed a debt you couldn't pay; He paid a debt He didn't owe.

You don't know my story. No, but He does. The Word exhorts us to forget those things of the past. If you're tied to your history, you cannot fulfill your destiny. Sever the anchor that keeps pulling you downward or backward. God has plans for a *masterpiece* in you. Rahab, the harlot, ended up in the lineage of Jesus; Peter denied Jesus, later he led the greatest crusade and 3,000 souls were saved (Acts 2:41).

We live in a world of racial divides, cultural differences, and stereotypes, but *in Christ, we are complete*. We're heirs and joint heirs with Christ; how glorious is that!

Walk with confidence in the authority and dominion He gave us. Refuse to be defined or marginalized. (*1 Peter 2:9-10 MSG).* Do not settle for less than ***all*** you're created to be. Occupy your God-ordained position, seated together ***in Christ*** above circumstances (Ephesians 2:6). Value Eternal things (*1 Timothy 6:11-12).* We're spiritual beings having a human experience.

You're a new creation; you're ***not*** inferior or worth-less, *YOU* are blessed and highly favored by God. Live like it!

Prayer

Father, thank you for choosing us before the foundation of the earth. We are Royalty, in Jesus' Name. Amen.

Monica Case Williams

VICTORIOUS LIVING

An Open Invitation

"Let us therefore come boldly to the throne of grace, that we may obtain mercy and find grace to help in time of need."

--Hebrews 4:16

Few of us have seen an earthly throne firsthand, let alone approached one. Our concept of what a throne is like comes largely from children's literature or movies. And even if we have seen a real throne, it was probably distant and forbidding. On my first visit to London, England, seeing Buckingham Palace was high on my list of things to do and experience. I hoped to see Queen Elizabeth's palace and possibly even to see inside and catch a glimpse of her throne. But the day I got there, I was disappointed, confined to a look at the palace from the outside with along the hundreds of fellow tourists, confined by a high fence and a large, imposing gate that implicitly said, "Keep out."

How different it is in God's Kingdom! Our scripture verse for today invites us into God's throne room with no restrictions. We can all be grateful that His throne of grace which is open twenty-four hours of the day, offers an invitation to all. What a change from the experience of the Old Testament! When God visited the children of Israel at Sinai (Exodus 19), His presence was so awesome that they were sternly warned to follow the specific instructions given by Moses, and not to 'draw near.' Later, when the high priest was given exclusive, privileged access and went past the second veil into the Holy of Holies to offer sacrifice for the sins of the people, his visits were restricted to once a year. But Christ's death on Calvary changed all that. Hallelujah! The veil has been removed (See Matthew

27:51) and access was opened to all into 'a new and living way'. We are all invited into God's throne room to receive mercy and to find help for our various needs.

Take time today to reflect on the privilege that is now ours. No high priest is needed because we have Jesus as our Advocate. We can come anytime with any need. Consider Isaiah 55: 1, Matthew 11: 28, John 7: 37, Revelation 22: 17. No matter what you are facing today, approach His throne to find the welcome that awaits you and the promise of the assistance of which you have been assured. Come boldly; come expectantly.

Prayer

"Just as I am, Thou wilt receive,

Will welcome, pardon, cleanse, relieve;

Because Thy promise I believe,

O Lamb of God, I come! I come!"

--Charlotte Elliott

Sheila Hoyte

Pave the Way for Victory

"Listen to my words, Lord, consider my lament. Hear my cry for help, my king and my God, for to you I pray. In the morning, Lord, you hear my voice; in the morning I lay my requests before you and wait expectantly. For you are not a God who is pleased with wickedness; with you evil people are not welcome."

--Psalm 5:1-4 *NIV*

It is a daunting thought when you realize that you have the power to make your day, week, month, or year a victorious one. Your words are like seeds and when you declare victory, favor and blessing, you will reap a harvest of victory, favor and blessing in return.

The Psalmist David declare: *"In the morning, Lord, you hear my voice; in the morning I lay my requests before you and wait expectantly"* verse 3. The word expectantly could be substituted with words like: hopeful, excited, eager. David knew that once he expressed his thoughts and desire to God, his faithful Father would lend an ear to his cry, and so he eagerly waited with excitement to see what and how God was going to turn his day around.

Did you know that every morning you have the opportunity to set the tone for your whole day? Yes, when you put God first and decide to go out with a grateful attitude and a positive frame of mind, not only will you feel better, but you're going to draw the good things of God to yourself. You are paving the way for success and victory. But if you get up thinking, "Life's a drag, nothing good ever happens to me. It's going to be a lousy day," then you are going to attract defeat, failure, and mediocrity.

Your words have power. No matter what you may be

facing today, the words of your mouth can help set the course for either your victory or defeat. You have to choose to set your day in the right direction. Find something to thank God for, even if you have to make a list of all the good things in your life and post it on your bathroom mirror. Even when challenges and obstacles arise, you have to rise up and say, "If God is for me, who can be against me." As you continually choose to set your mind on God first thing in the morning, you'll pave the way to victory and enjoy the good things He has in store for you!

Prayer

Lord, teach me to lift my voice to You early in the morning so You can order my steps throughout the day. Thank you for Your faithful hand that leads and directs Your children. Amen.

Rosalind Coltherst-Smallhorne

Spending Time in the Word of God

"Thy word have I hid in mine heart that I might not sin against thee."

--Psalm 119: 11

In this high technological era, the Bible is on phones, laptops and other devices. The Word of God is now easily accessible, not just in hard copy form.

A word of caution, when going out, keep a hard copy, technology fails, and you may need to witness to someone. Just don't read the Bible on the 'run'. Spend time and cultivate a discipline in studying the Word. Endeavor to start the day in God's Word and use devotionals and Bible aids to help in assimilating same.

This is not easy, and I speak from a personal struggle. The enemy presents distractions in the form of exercise sessions, breaking news reports, household chores, and deadlines.

One of our church's speakers shared that while in high school, there was a written mantra, 'No Bible No Breakfast'. Certainly, this was a positive reinforcement for developing young strong Christians.

The Word of God is vital for our Christian walk and facing daily challenges. Psalm 119: 89 states, "Forever, O Lord, thy word is settled in heaven." Given this, it is imperative we have not just head knowledge, but the Word must resonate in our hearts and souls. As such, quality time must be spent in the Word of God.

Have a missionary zeal, in sharing devotionals with your listing on the social network. Oftentimes, this is the only means through which persons have contact with Jesus

Christ of Nazareth.

Prayer

Dear Lord, we come to you asking for a mind to truly worship You. Help us to get into the habit of studying the Word, to repel satan's fiery darts and grow in You. 1 Peter 2: 2: "As newborn babes, desire the sincere milk of the word, that ye may grow thereby." In Jesus' Name. Amen.

Andrea Dunk

The Power of Spoken Blessings: Part I

"Then God blessed them, and God said to them, "Be fruitful and multiply; fill the earth and subdue it; have dominion over the fish of the sea, over the birds of the air, and over every living thing that moves on the earth."

--Genesis 1:28 *NKJV*

Did you know that you have a spiritual birthright you likely have not yet received? It is a birthright of verbal blessings (also known as the Family Blessing), and it holds the key to having a fulfilling journey through life. We read of different kinds of blessing in the Bible. However, your birthright blessing is yours just because you were born. There is nothing you have to do to earn it because it is your Heavenly Father's gift of love that He designed for you as His offspring.

God introduced and modeled this birthright blessing in His first encounter with humanity (Adam) at creation. While Genesis 1:28 is often referred to as our dominion mandate, it is so much more. Genesis 1:28 is first and foremost a blessing of intentional words that transferred divine empowerment and favor upon Adam's identity and destiny at the very beginning of his existence.

You and I were meant to receive similar divine transfers that equip us for a prosperous and fulfilling journey through life. It's not too late if you have missed your blessing birthright! I was fifty years old when I recovered mine. Because the spoken blessing is a spiritual reality and because we share God's Spirit essence, we can transcend time to recover that which our spirit has been longing for. Ephesians 1:3 is good news:

> *"Blessed be the God and Father of our Lord Jesus Christ, who has blessed us with every spiritual blessing in the heavenly places in Christ."*

You can experience the joy of recovering your spiritual birthright and in turn help others to do the same. You are rightly positioned by God in your family and in other relationships to speak intentional words that transform and shape lives. There is a divine urgency if children and future generations are going to fulfill God's purposes. We cannot afford for them to struggle through life because of a blessing deficit.

> *So, today I bless you with activated faith to recover every spiritual blessing that Father God ordained for you to possess from the time of conception in your mother's womb to your present stage of life and beyond. As God's beloved, you have what it takes to prosper in your ordained identity and destiny. I bless you to be a blessing, especially to the younger generations.*

Prayer

Heavenly Father, I am grateful for your relentless love and grace expressed through the Cross so that I do not have to live without the blessings you designed for me as a birthright gift. I now activate my faith to recover all through Jesus Christ. Thank you for empowering me to be your mouthpiece for blessing others. Amen.

Rev. Marva Tyndale

The Power of Spoken Blessings: Part II

And Esau said to his father, "Have you only one blessing, my father? Bless me—me also, O my father!" And Esau lifted up his voice and wept."

--Genesis 27:38 *NKJV*

Today's verse picks up Esau's gut-wrenching response after Jacob tricked their father, Isaac, and received the words of blessing that he had intended to speak over Esau. We can't help but ask, what is it about a blessing that would cause a grown man at the age of forty to weep so bitterly because words intended for him were spoken to someone else?

In ancient Jewish culture, words of blessing were coveted above material wealth. Esau had grown up with verbal blessings as a way of life; a legacy of his grandfather Abraham whom God had called and blessed (See Gen 12: 1-3; 22:17-18). He would have embraced the thinking of his time that whoever had the blessing had it all. He knew that the spoken blessing had supernatural power to thrust him forward with empowerment to prosper in his identity and destiny. He would have believed what is said about spoken blessings even to this day—blessings empower us to prosper in spite of our weaknesses, but when we don't receive them, we struggle through life although we may be gifted or talented.

The outcome of the life of these two brothers certainly validates the transformative power of a verbal blessing. The blessing that Jacob received never stopped working through the many trials and encounters of his life. The words spoken in faith by his father, Isaac, became an instrument in the hand of God that transformed Jacob's nature from the "deceiver Jacob" to the "prince Israel." The blessing helped to thrust him into his destiny as father of the Twelve Tribes of Israel.

This same transformative power is available to you, and your Heavenly Father wants to activate it in your life from this day forward. It is my privilege, on behalf of Father God to release in your life the blessing that Jacob spoke over the two sons of Joseph, a blessing that remains at the heart of the Jewish culture even to this day. The blessing is based on the meaning of the names of the two boys: Manasseh, which means "making forgetful," and Ephraim, which means "fruitfulness" (See Genesis 41:50-52; 48:18-20).

> *"May God make you like Ephraim and Manasseh—may He cause you to forget the pain of your past, including the pain of your father's house, and may He make you fruitful and prosperous in the future."*

Prayer

Heavenly Father, thank you for releasing this blessing of transformation over me. As you did for Jacob, I ask you to let the power of this blessing continue to work in my life until I am shaped and formed in the image of Christ. I believe that you have sent this blessing to empower me to prosper in my identity and destiny. I receive all it is sent to do, in Jesus' name. Amen.

Rev. Marva Tyndale

Your Blessing Birthright

Then God blessed them, and God said to them, "Be fruitful and multiply; fill the earth and subdue it; have dominion over the fish of the sea, over the birds of the air, and over every living thing that moves on the earth."

--Genesis 1:28 *NKJV*

Did you know that you have a spiritual birthright you likely have not yet received? It is a birthright of verbal blessings (also known as the Family Blessing), and it holds the key to having a fulfilling journey through life. We read of different kinds of blessing in the Bible; however, your birthright blessing is yours just because you were born. There is nothing you have to do to earn it because it is your Heavenly Father's gift of love that He designed for you as His offspring.

God introduced and modeled this birthright blessing in His first encounter with humanity (Adam) at creation. While Genesis 1:28 is often referred to as our Dominion Mandate, it is so much more. Genesis 1:28 is first and foremost a blessing of intentional words that transferred divine empowerment and favor upon Adam's identity and destiny at the very beginning of his existence.

You and I were meant to receive similar divine transfers that equip us for a prosperous and fulfilling journey through life. It's not too late if you have missed your blessing birthright! I was fifty years old when I recovered mine. Because the spoken blessing is a spiritual reality and because we share God's Spirit essence, we can transcend time to recover that which our spirit has been longing for. Ephesians 1:3 is good news: *"Blessed be the God and Father of our Lord Jesus Christ, who has blessed us with every spiritual blessing in the heavenly places in Christ."*

You can experience the joy of recovering your spiritual birthright and in turn help others to do the same. You are rightly positioned by God in your family and in other relationships to speak intentional words that transform and shape lives. There is a divine urgency if children and future generations are going to fulfill God's purposes. We cannot afford for them to struggle through life because of a blessing deficit.

> *So, today I bless you with activated faith to recover every spiritual blessing that Father God ordained for you to possess from the time of conception in your mother's womb to your present stage of life and beyond. As God's beloved, you have what it takes to prosper in your ordained identity and destiny. I bless you to be a blessing, especially to the younger generations.*

Prayer

Heavenly Father, I am grateful for your relentless love and grace expressed through the Cross so that I do not have to live without the blessings you designed for me as a birthright gift. I now activate my faith to recover all through Jesus Christ. Thank you for empowering me to be your mouthpiece for blessing others. Amen.

Rev. Marva Tyndale

Get Your Power Up

"Now unto Him who is able to do...according to the power that works in you."

--Ephesians 3:20

A casual relationship with God will not bring growth and deliverance to the believer. We must get plugged in and stay connected through a disciplined prayer life and studying God's Word. If a building is wired for electricity, you must flick the switch to get power. Consequently, you must activate the spiritual switch to experience the manifestation of God's power in your life. If you are praying and not getting the desired results, check your connection to the power source – it's *"according to the power that works in you."*

Knowledge is power! God has made every provision through the Holy Spirit for us to live powerful, victorious lives. When we study the Word, God reveals precious truths to us about Himself and who we are in Him. When we discover the truth that we are kingdom citizens, understand the rights and privileges that belong to us, we become dangerous to the kingdom of darkness.

When Pharaoh told Moses everyone could leave Egypt to go and worship but they should leave their livestock, Moses told him, "… not one hoof would be left behind…" (Exodus 10:26), Pharaoh relented. Luke 10:16 says the Holy Spirit has given us power and authority to trample on serpents and scorpions. We have the authority to defeat the evil schemes, assignments, and devastations the devil sends against us and our loved ones.

Many years ago, we were faced with a potentially devastating situation if we did not have God's intervention. As I prayed to God in earnest, I dropped my Bible on the ground, took off my shoes, stood on the Bible and declared, "Father, You told me to stand on your Word and I am literally standing on it, honor your Word in my life." The power was activated, and He brought a miraculous deliverance to us. Hallelujah!

The power is already in you but may be dormant. Activate the power and experience remarkable victories in your life.

Prayer

Father, help us to recognize that the Holy Spirit is at work in our lives. We are not victims; we are victorious through your anointing, in Jesus' Name. Amen.

Monica Case Williams

Refuse to Back Up. Keep Fighting!

"Not that we are sufficient of ourselves to think anything as of ourselves; but our sufficiency is of God."

--2 Corinthians 3: 5

The enemy's tactics are not anything new. In fact, if you are a student of the Word at all, you can see that all his schemes fall into one main category and that is the category of Deception.

He uses outright trickery, shocking us into a state of fear, doubt, nearsightedness or outright blindness to the truth and at other times he uses intimidation or bravado which is also rooted in lies.

Intimidation seeks to silence and steal one's voice, confidence, and courage, inducing a sense of uselessness and inferiority! It's all a smoke screen -always was and always will be!

David wouldn't have it. Goliath threw every insult he could to cause David to cower and retreat -

Neither would Elijah when the Prophets of Baal tried to intimidate him by the obvious deficiencies of his circumstances at the time.

Isn't that how it is with you and I?. There is always a circumstance or a situation looming when the enemy rears his head! But like David and Elijah and countless others who've proven God faithful, they stood their ground - not in their own determination. Their determination was stabilized by the One who had proven Himself faithful, on-time and victorious!

We all have circumstances and they are all so real, sometimes very overwhelming and beyond our capabilities or resources or ability. I remember as a kid, I would have a game plan if I knew if I was going to be challenged to a fight. I would make up my mind to keep swinging! Yep! Keep getting up and keep swinging; that is somewhat of what I find myself doing right now! I defy the tactics of the enemy by getting back up and choosing to believe the report of the Lord! Refusing to back up for fear of ________________, you fill in the blank! This scripture is helping me this week! A friend shared it with me and as I prayed, it's giving me life!!!!

"Such is the confidence that we have through Christ toward God. Not that we are sufficient in ourselves to claim anything as coming from us, but our sufficiency is from God, who has made us sufficient to be ministers of a new covenant, not of the letter but of the Spirit. For the letter kills, but the Spirit gives life" (2 Corinthians 3:4-6).

Prayer

Heavenly Father, I have confidence in You that You are able to lift me up when the enemy tries to knock me down. Thank You for the strength to keep getting up. Amen.

Rev. Alicia Morgan

Thy Will Be Done

"And we know that all things work together for good to them that love God, to them who are called according to His purpose."

--Romans 8:28

A mother knelt praying at the bedside of her seven-year-old son who was ill with a rare virus. Some eight years ago, she had knelt at her own bedside praying that she would conceive. God had granted her request.

As she knelt praying at the son's bedside, she fell into a trance and had a vision in which God cured her son, but as the vision continued, she saw herself kneeling again in prayer but this time it was at a prison. In the vision, the son who had been healed twelve years later, had lived a life of disobedience and riotous living and was now in prison on a murder charge. She awoke from the trance, looked on her seven-year-old son barely conscious, folded his arms across his chest and said, "God, your will be done." Her son died at age seven, innocent enough to be part of God's Kingdom, instead of at nineteen where the vision indicated he would be a murderer.

There are several scriptures concerning the Will of God. Biblical scholars pontificate and debate various issues.

1. Is it necessary to say the "perfect will of God or just "The will of God" since God is perfect, so His will is perfect?
2. Is it necessary after an intercessory prayer to close by saying, "Your will be done," or since God grants according to His will, it is understood that when we ask, we already know it is according to His will?

The important thing is that it is not about us, but rather of Him with regard to the purpose for our lives. Even Jesus Christ the Son of God in the Garden of Gethsemane prayed according to Luke 22:42, "Father if it is Your will …nevertheless not my will, but Yours be done." The will of God in sync with our conscience being unctionized by the Holy Spirit keeps us on the path of righteousness.

God gives us the option to choose but He provides:

1) His blessed Holy Spirit.
2) His Word
3) Our friends, mentors or relatives
4) A built-in conscience to help us in our decision-making when we truly accept Him as Lord and Savior.

We are human and we err, so we must be persistent in applying Ephesians 6:10-18 to our lives. Not all of us will get a "direct word" as the mother in the story did. But if we truly accept God as Savior and Lord and realize it is not about us, we will always say, "Thy Will Be Done."

Prayer

Let your will be done in our lives, Lord. Let us see Your Hand at work at all times. Amen.

JAT

PRAYER

How Should I Pray?

"Our Father which art in Heaven."

--Matthew 6: 9-10

Prayer is the most vital connection that we have between man and God. It is the source of the believer's strength. It bridges the gap that separates us from our Father. When the disciples wanted to know how to pray, Jesus so eloquently taught them to pray. It begins by acknowledging God as our Father. Not just His Father, their Father, but our Father, which includes you and me. So many feel disconnected from their earthly father, but there is an unchangeable Heaven Father who always claims us and embraces us as His own.

The Lord's Prayer speaks to our relationship with our Father. As a child comes humbly to his earthly father asking for help, so we too can approach our Heavenly Father in an attitude of submission to make our request known. It is always so good to know that God is our Father, a Father of love and mercy. Regardless of our color, race and nationality, He means the same to each of us as John 3:16 declares, "For God so loved the world."

The Lord's Prayer, "Our Father," gives us a connection with every other person. We have the same Father. What does that mean? In an age when we are so divided, it is good to know that we are connected through our Father in Heaven. We stand on equal footing in His presence. The ground is level with God.

Do you sometimes think that God favors others above you? Be reminded that He belongs to all of us and to each He demonstrates love, care redemption and forgiveness. What a God!!!

Prayer

Our Father, thank you for being our Father. You have always shown Fatherly love, even when I wander away from you. Thank you for always being there for me. Amen.

Beverly Coker

Communication Through Prayer

"And whatsoever ye shall ask in my name, that will I do, that the Father may be glorified in the Son. If ye shall ask any thing in my name, I will do it."

--John 14:13-14

Communication is an important subject in our society. Communication with God empowers you with grace and ability to positively impact lives. Communing with God is absolutely necessary for spiritual growth and wellbeing; it is called prayer. Prayer is communication with God. In prayer, you verbalize your petitions and rehearse God's promises, which build/increase your faith to believe. Prayer brings the power of God into action. As you go before the Lord:

- **Pray Confidently**. In Matthew19:26 *NIV*, the Bible tells us that nothing is impossible with God. These are not man's words; it is a promise from the mouth of Jesus. With that in mind, you can approach prayer with confidence in God's authority. People break promises, or change their minds according to their feelings, but you can depend on, and be confident in, the authenticity of God's Word.
- **Pray in the Authority of Christ.** (John 14: 13-14) "...Ask in my name... *You may ask me for anything... I will do it"*. Name matters. The Name of Jesus has power and authority both in heaven and on earth. Therefore, pray in the Name of Jesus. His Name activates the force and authority of heaven into your situation. In Acts 3, Peter healed a crippled beggar. *"Silver or gold I do not have... In the name of*

Jesus Christ of Nazareth, walk." By faith, bring your petitions to Jesus. In the authority of Jesus, break strongholds. (Read: Luke 10: 19; 2 Cor. 10: 4).

- **Pray Continually.** Pray before making decisions and develop a lifestyle of fellowship with Christ through prayer. ***"Pray without ceasing"*** (1Thessalonians 5:17). If you are troubled, downhearted, fearful or confused about life's overwhelming problems, take heart. Pray in faith believing, rely on God's promises and wait for Him. He will answer.

Prayer

Father, in the Name of Jesus, I thank you for the desire to communicate with you in prayer.

Rev. Lenore Kidd

Are you an Intercessor?

"Praying always with all prayers and supplication in the Spirit, and watching thereunto with all perseverance and supplication for all saints."

--Ephesians 6:18

Prayer should be a vital part of our daily lives. It gets us through difficult situations and helps us to face the challenges of life. Without prayer and God's intervention, we would absolutely fall apart. However, there are times when our personal prayers seem insufficient. That's when we call on others to pray for us. The people who approach God on our behalf are called **Intercessors**. Intercession is saying a prayer on behalf of another person, using your influence to make someone in authority do something favorable for that individual. In essence, we approach God as mediators, a go-between for help to solve someone else's problems.

So often, I need people to stand in the gap for me when I am unable to do so myself. All of us need the divine intervention that occurs when people collectively approach God on our behalf.

Paul reminds us, "that, first of all, supplications, prayers, intercessions and giving of thanks, be made, for all men" (1 Timothy 2:1). I have often heard of people who interceded for someone, known and unknown, who at a crucial time needed God's coverage and intervention. Prayer changes things and intercessors change life's situations, circumstances, and bring about positive results.

Let each of us endeavor to intercede for someone besides ourselves. Abraham interceded for Sodom and Gomorrah, and God spared the cities' ten godly people because

Abraham interceded. When Peter was imprisoned, the church interceded, and Peter was miraculously delivered. Intercession can change the course of someone's life. However, it is hard work. It is indeed, a battle that requires commitment and patience.

Do you know that you can intercede for someone in a distant land, like a missionary or people who are falsely imprisoned for the sake of Christ? Your prayer for them can make a difference. Someone is depending on your prayers today to change the course of their situation. The church needs intercessors; we need one another. Will you be one? Jesus interceded for us, that is why He spent so much time talking to His Father.

Prayer

Heavenly Father, give us the urge to advocate for someone today. There might be one person who cannot come to you for themselves. Help us to stand in the gap for that person who so desperately needs you. Amen.

Beverly Coker

Prayer

"Therefore, I say unto you, 'What things soever ye desire, when ye pray, believe that ye receive them, and ye shall have them.'"

--Mark 11:24

PRAYER IS COMUNICATION: It is the means by which believers communicate with God, Our Father. Good communication involves speaking and listening; therefore, when we pray, we MUST spend time in LISTENING to Him. He is not our equal; we must honor or adore Him when we pray. Jesus taught us in the model prayer, "Our Father which art in heaven, hallowed be thy name" (Luke 11:26 *KJV*).

PRAYER REQUIRES FAITH: The verse starts off with "therefore," meaning, it's connected to a previous verse, which says that you should not have doubt in your heart when you pray, and you will have what you ask for. We should pray in faith and God will hear and answer our prayers.

BELIEVE that what we ask for, we receive. Believing comes before receiving. Consequently, when we pray, we know that we receive. Therefore, we should move forward in faith. There is no need to wait for the manifestation. We walk by FAITH and not by SIGHT. (2 Corinthians 5:7 KJV).

ASK ACCORDING TO HIS WILL: When we pray in faith, believe in our hearts and pray according to His will, we have the confidence that encourages us to go forward.
PRAYER REQUIRES RELATIONSHIP: When we pray to God, we must have a good relationship with Him and with others in order to receive answers to our prayers. (John 15:7: Mark 11: 25 *KJV*).

HINDRANCES TO ANSWERED PRAYERS: Some things that prevent positive outcomes to our prayers are:

a) Unbelief: the scripture tells us when we pray, we should believe, and we will have them.
b) Our prayers are not according to God's will.
c) There is unforgiveness in our hearts (Mark 11:26).

Jesus tells us that if we do not forgive others then our Heavenly Father will not forgive us.

Prayer

In the Name of Jesus, I come to you, God. You are Holy, Righteous, and Faithful. Thank You for your forgiveness, for your love and for answering my prayers according to your will as I endeavor to live in loving relationship with You and others. In Jesus' name I pray. Amen.

Rev. Nessa C. Oram-Edwards

Pray or be Prey

"Finally, be strong in the Lord and in the strength of his might. Put on the whole armor of God, that you may be able to stand against the schemes of the devil. For we do not wrestle against flesh and blood, but against the rulers, against the authorities, against the cosmic powers over this present darkness, against the spiritual forces of evil in the heavenly places. Therefore, take up the whole armor of God, that you may be able to withstand in the evil day, and having done all, to stand firm."

--Ephesians 6: 10-13

"Pray at all times in the Spirit, with all prayer and supplication. To that end keep alert with all perseverance, making supplication for all the saints."

--Ephesians 6: 18

There are spiritual forces fighting against us, intending to destroy us. The fact that they are always *preying* on us should motivate us to *pray*. We are informed of the intensity of this fight and are encouraged to be properly prepared for it. The secret for success and the key for victory is prayer. You cannot win without prayer, and with prayer you cannot loose.

We must recognize and identify who we are really fighting. That supervisor, co-worker, neighbor or family member that are filled with evil intentions, is not the real enemy. We cannot see the real enemy with our physical eyes. They manifest themselves through the people around us, but the true war is against unseen forces.

"Against the cosmic powers over this present darkness, against the spiritual forces of evil in the heavenly places" (Ephesians 6:12).

At first glance, this might sound downright scary. How is it then that we are not afraid? Herein lies our confidence. We are told how to prepare for the fight. We should *"put on the whole armor of God."* Pray to be clothed in our spiritual battle attire. That which hold all these pieces together and make them effectively work for us, is prayer.

> *"Praying at all times in the Spirit, with all prayer and supplication. To that end keep alert with all perseverance, making supplication for all the saints."* (Ephesians 6:18)

Prayer

Heavenly Father, you have already given us victory over the powers of darkness. May we not be a prey for the enemy but be encouraged and motivated to pray that we would see the manifestation of this victory in Jesus' name. Amen.
Rev. Charlton Daley

Call Upon Me

"Call upon me in the day of trouble; I shall rescue you, and you will honor me."

--Psalm 50:15

Sometimes, God allows us to experience times of distress so we can call upon him for help. It is during these times that we prove God to be reliable. He always delivers those who put their trust in Him, giving them an opportunity to glorify and honor His name.

In July of 1988, seven days after giving birth to my fifth child, I was in the bathroom around 6:00 a.m. preparing to brush my teeth when I heard the most gut-wrenching scream coming from my eldest daughter. I spun around to see what the cause of her scream was and came face to face with three masked men bearing guns. My initial response was fear, but I quickly realized that I was alone with three of my children and needed divine intervention.

I called upon Jesus in a loud voice, and His presence instantaneously filled the room. My fear was replaced with boldness as I watched the gunmen tremble in their boots.

God gave me the boldness to minister to them before they left my home that morning. He reassured me that when we call upon Him in times of trouble, He will always be there to rescue us.

Prayer

Father, we praise and glorify your name today because of who you are. We are thankful that you are reliable, and we can always call upon you in times of trouble. In spite of the predicaments we face today, we are confident that you will rescue us, and we in turn will honor and glorify your name. Thanks for hearing and answering our prayers. In Jesus' precious name we pray. Amen.

Rev. Sandra Rhone

OVERCOMING CHALLENGES

Surviving the Night Season

"Nevertheless God, that comforteth those that are cast down comforted us by the coming of Titus."

--2 Corinthian 7:6

In this scripture, Paul shared with the Corinthian church the conflicts he faced in Macedonia. Paul was being transparent when he shared with the Corinthians the struggles he faced in Macedonia. Passion Translation records, "We were restless and exhausted; troubles met us at every turn. Outwardly I faced conflicts and inwardly emotional turmoil" (2 Corinthians 7: 5). Trouble has a way of leaving us exhausted by the physical and emotional pain we are forced to endure. In this state of despondency, many question the Sovereign God. How do we find comfort in pain and suffering?

In our darkest moments, in our night season, we can take comfort in a God who promises not to leave us nor forsake us. We can be "more than conquerors through Him who loved us" (Romans 8:37). He is with us even in our suffering.

Everyone encounters tough times; no one is exempt from the pitfalls of depression and despair. Suffering sometimes robs us of our ability to think clearly, to realize that suffering builds character and character gives hope.

It is reassuring to know that even in our moments of suffering, God is ever present, and He provides a way of escape. We escape when we spend quality time in the presence of God through prayer. James reminds us that the "effectual fervent prayer of a righteous man availeth much" (1:16). Prayer is powerful and through it we are able to connect with a God of tender mercies and compassion.

Like many of us, Paul might have reached a point of brokenness in his interaction with the Macedonians, "But God, who always knows how to encourage the depressed encouraged us greatly by the arrival of Titus" (2 Corinthians 7:6 *TPT)*. God sometimes sends comfort through people, fellow believers to lighten our load when we are overwhelmed by circumstances. As believers, even in our night season we can rejoice and praise God, for He is the Father of tender mercies and the God of endless comfort.

God provides unlimited resources to strengthen us in all our struggles. David found comfort in stating, "In all my affliction I find great comfort in your promises, for they have kept me alive!" (Psalm 119:50 *TPT*). To whom do you turn when your back is against the wall and the night season has come upon you? Hope thou in God. *"God you're such a safe and powerful place to find refuge! You're a proven help in time of trouble more than enough and always available whenever I need you"* (Psalm 46:1 *TPT*).

Prayer

I am so grateful that I can turn to you when I am in trouble. You always send hope and light to see me through my circumstances. Amen.

Beverly Coker

Dealing with Stress

"Set your eyes on the works of God and Trust Him."

--Psalms 11-112

Each day, we have the opportunity to think about the impressive works of God and His sovereignty, glory, and strength. We are privileged to be able to engage in conversations with God through prayer and meditation; however, more often than not, we focus our attention on the challenges, situations, and circumstances that concern us.

We put a great deal of energy into worrying and stressing over life's problems. It is a natural tendency of human beings. We do this, even when we know that worrying does not help. We focus on our issues so intensely that we often begin to experience emotional, psychological, and physical stress in our bodies.

The stress is so unbearable at times that our bodies become over polluted with an abundance of adrenaline and cortisol hormones. Physiologically, our breathing becomes labored, our hearts race, and our brains begin to lose their capacity to analyze, process, and send accurate messages throughout our bodies.

In essence, our executive functioning capacity becomes overwhelmed with the flood of emotions we experience when we are under stress or pressure. With this focus, our perspectives undergo a shaping process that often makes us view our situations as being hopeless, insurmountable, and unconquerable.

On the other hand, when we shift our eyes unto the works of God as mentioned in Psalm 111, we cannot help but begin to think of the greatness and power of our God. As we continue to meditate on His goodness, mercy, and love toward us, a sense of security cascades over us, dispelling the dark clouds that usually accompany stress. Moreover, as we consider His sovereignty, glory, and strength, our perspectives begin to bend toward hopefulness and seeing our situations as surmountable and conquerable.

Also, when our minds focus on our Lord and His great power and divine characteristics, serotonin and dopamine hormones flood our bodies, showering us with pleasure and great joy. As our minds begin to clear and our sense of security returns, we typically find that praises naturally start to bubble up within us, and our souls are refreshed and revived. As we SET our eyes on the works, sovereignty, power, and strength of our God, our situations lose their ability to ignite worry in us. They become devoid of the power to manipulate our senses. They begin to diminish in size and potency in the face of God's active presence in our lives. At these times, we are reminded to trust God and believe Him when He said that He would never leave us or forsake us.

Prayer

God, thank you for your word of comfort, encouragement, and motivation. Thank you for the gift of Holy Spirit who can remind me to trust you and to fix my eyes on your works, your sovereignty, power, and strength. Please help me to faithfully cast my cares upon you and not let me keep my eyes on the problems I face each day. Thank you for your graciousness toward me to remind me of these truths today. In Jesus' name I pray. Amen.

Dr. Alice Farrell

Tested and Triumphant

"Remember my chains. Grace be with you."

--Colossians 4:18

Testing is a natural part of life and it comes to everyone sooner or later. It's not something we embrace – whether it is of our own making or through uncontrolled circumstances. How do you react during those times of testing? How can you change your attitude or behavior and grow from your experiences?

Never lose sight of the fact that God is ABSOLUTELY for You. There are promises at the end of the test, but we must endure the process to gain those promises. Could it be that God is processing you to take you into Greatness?

Social media has provided a platform for people to openly share some of the most personal things and events about themselves – grab attention at any cost. There is an increasing appetite to "tell my story" to every, and anyone. There's an old hymn, "I Love to Tell the Story," but it's the story of Jesus' redemptive love for a lost world, to heal, deliver, and set us free.

Paul emphasizes in the Book of Colossians that Christ is first and foremost, and that our lives should reflect that priority as well. Paul, writing from prison, further gave instructions on how to live a Godly and victorious life and *specifically* appealed to husbands, wives, children, and masters. This was like a father writing to his children, exhorting them to keep the faith and grow in grace. Tucked in the final verse of the last chapter, Paul so poignantly closed his letter with – "**Remember my chains**" and pronounced a blessing, "Grace be with you."

This same Paul who endured unimaginable hardships (See 2 Corinthians 11:23-33) victoriously proclaimed at the end of his life, *"I have finished the course, I have kept the faith, henceforth there is laid up for me a Crown."* His chains were a badge of honor. Paul was God's warrior – tested and triumphant! How about you?

Prayer

Father, thank you for your unfailing love, your grace, and how you perfect that which concerns me. Strengthen me with might on the inner man to glorify your Name in my life. Amen.

Monica Case Williams

Say It Out Loud: "God's Got This!"

"So do not fear, for I am with you; do not be dismayed, for I am your God. I will strengthen you and help you; I will uphold you with my righteous right hand."

--Isaiah 41:10

He is the same yesterday, today and forever more.

Are you going through an insurmountable experience? Or have you ever been through something that seemed insurmountable at the time?

Wow! I am so glad that you are reading this right now, and I am so glad that I have the privilege of sharing with you, right where you are. Let me reassure you: God did it then and, without a doubt, He's Got This Now!

I will tell you a story. Just recently, we experienced a major rain storm. During the wee hours of that night, our family realized there was a significant leak, water literally flowing like a tap from our roof. The water leaked into three floors of our home. To say that this was alarming would be mild. Yet, we also realized something that was also deeply sobering.

After a bit of investigation, what would you know? We discovered that the leak was in fact several years old and over time had significantly damaged the walls. The normal seasons of rain and snow were just not enough to make it visible or make us aware that we were breathing in mold that had made a home in the moist walls. You see, the very storm none of us were happy to have in our midst was the turning point! That storm, in fact, gave us the critical awareness we needed to restore the structure of our home; back to what was originally intended!

Here's the truth, far beyond what seemed humanly logical before this revelation, I now thanked God for the storm. I found myself saying, "Daddy, you did this for us?" In awe, we were indeed so grateful that this storm was in fact God's signal to us of needed restoration, and the key needed to open the door to this restoration.

TODAY, WOULD YOU DARE TO CHALLENGE YOURSELF TO KNOW THE LOVE AND FAITHFULNESS OF GOD THAT PASSES KNOWLEDGE?

I'll ask again, are you going through something that seems insurmountable?

Your prayer today is simple as a breath, yet so very reassuring. Sometimes that's all we need to release simple faith.

Prayer

Say it out aloud: "God's Got This!" Believe it deep within: "God's Got This!"

Andrea Boweya

It is in His Hands

"And the Lord said, I have surely seen the affliction of my people which are in Egypt, and have heard their cry by reason of their taskmasters; for I know their sorrows."

--Exodus 3: 7-8

Allegories are tales or stories that are not necessarily true, but instead serve to illustrate a point. One such allegory tells the story of a man living by a river in a flood prone area. He was chopping fire wood when he inexplicably felt the unction to go inside, just in time to hear on the radio a flash flood warning for his area. He went back outside and later the rain started. He saw a boat going down the river and people beckoning him to join them.

Later on, when heavy rains flooded his house, he sought refuge on his roof and a helicopter flew over, but he made no attempt to signal them. His house was completely submerged, and he drowned. He went to Heaven where he promptly asked God, "Why did You not save me from drowning?" God said to him, "I warned you once and sent for you twice."

God sees, hears, and knows about our circumstances as He told Moses in verses 7-8. He tries to get our attention as he did with Moses and the burning bush or by the radio broadcast as the allegory suggests. Sometimes, like Moses, we are reluctant to take on the task or we want to wait for some miraculous, grand, instant solution.

The "I Am Who I Am" does not only see, hear, and know our situation, He has a plan. Due to non-adherence or disobedience, the plan may be delayed and can be denied through lack of obedience. We need to discern, acknowledge, and obey His plan and know the outcome is in His Hands – but obedience is key.

Prayer

Lord, teach me to trust you at all times, even when I cannot see the outcome. I thank you that you always have a plan. Amen.

JAT

When You Don't Understand!

"Did I not tell you that if you believed, you would see the glory of God?"

--John 11:40

Mary and Martha could not understand what their Lord was doing. Both of them said to Him, "Lord, if you had been here, my brother would not die." Their thoughts may have been, "Lord, we do not understand why you have stayed away so long? We do not understand how you could let death come to the man whom you loved! We do not understand how you could let sorrow and suffering ravage our lives when your presence might have stayed it all! Why did you not come? It is too late now, for already he has been dead 4 days!"

And to it all, Jesus had but one great truth:

> "You may not understand; but I tell you if you believe, you will see."

Abraham could not understand why God should ask the sacrifice of his son; but he trusted. And he saw the glory of God in the restoration of His love.

Joseph could not understand the cruelty of his brothers, the false witness of a deceitful woman, and the long years of an unjust imprisonment, but he trusted, and he saw, at last, the glory of God in it all.

And so perhaps in your life you say, "I do not understand why affliction has been permitted to smite me. I do not understand why blessings I so much need, are so long delayed."

You do not have to understand all God's ways with you.

He gave us His Word and the Holy Spirit to help us understand. You do not expect your child to understand everything, only believe. Someday you will see the glory of God in the things which you do not understand – we must trust Him.

Prayer

Lord, help me to trust you even when I do not understand. Amen.

Rev. Terry D. Joseph

When You Face Discouragement

"Nevertheless God, that comforteth those that are cast down, comforted us by the coming of Titus."

--2 Corinthians 7:6

What are you faced with today? All of us experience times of discouragement when we feel alone and downcast. The God of all comfort knows when to send people in our lives to help lift us out of situations. You do not have to be professionally trained to be a source of encouragement to someone. A word spoken in the right season, not being judgmental, but with compassion and care, can do much more than you could imagine. God puts friends in our lives to lift us out of seemingly devastating situations. The Lord sent Titus to comfort Paul. Indeed, we are our brothers' keepers, and love gives us the passion to carry each other's troubles (Galatians 6:2).

I have come to realize that no matter how impossible the circumstances seem, there is a way out. Begin to look to the hills from whence cometh your help (Psalm 121:1). E. Stanly Jones once said, "When life kicks you, let it kick you forward." Are you ready with the encouragement of others to rise up and move forward again? Do not allow the enemy of your soul to cause you to wallow in self-pity. There is help available. Reach out to someone, or more importantly, to the Higher power.

Your attitude and approach this day could be the change agent for tomorrow.

"Have not I commanded thee? Be strong and of a good courage; be not afraid, neither be thou dismayed: for the Lord thy God is with thee whithersoever thou goest." (Joshua 1:9).

Prayer

Heavenly Father, The God of all comfort, thank you for being there for me when I needed you the most. We are never without your everlasting arms. Amen.

Beverly Coker

When Life Happens

"And lo, I am with you always, even to the end of the age."

-- Matthew 28:20

Although a young child then, I remember vividly the night of the storm. The terrifying sounds of the fierce, unrelenting winds and driving rains that sounded like rushing waters. Fear gripped my heart. Weeping uncontrollably, I jumped in bed between my grandparents who comforted me. The storm did not cease for hours, but I was calmed by the presence of my loving, protective grandparents.

As I matured, other storms came, the kinds which assail us in the journey of life. Recently, a devastating storm struck our family. Our younger of two sons was taken from us suddenly and prematurely. The pain and grief are indescribable – the loss continues to penetrate our souls. There are days when we could not pray; just lift our thoughts to the God of all comfort and He bathes us with His presence. Then I remembered, the storm did not cease when I was cradled between my grandparents, but it was their presence, care and love that assured me of safety.

"Peace ***I leave*** with you, my peace ***I give*** to you. "

--John. 14:27

The Hurricane Season comes each year, and although it doesn't hit everywhere, it comes and brings devastation. It is said, the ship sinks when the water gets on the inside of the ship. We struggle, but we have determined not to allow grief to settle on the inside of our spirits. "Yea, though I walk ***through*** the valley . . . for you are with me;"

and thank God for a host of praying family and friends who carry us too.

So, what do we do when *"**life happens?**"*

We live in a sin-fallen world, so know that those times will come. We get anchored in the Word of God and stay covered by the blood of Jesus. Develop a deep, personal relationship with God, He can be trusted, and He really means it, ". . . lo I am with you **always** . . ." Safety is not the absence of trouble; safety is the presence of Jesus in the midst of the storm. As the song says, "You are my strength, strength like no other, reaches me."

Prayer

Thank You Father, who remembers our frame that we are dust. When we are terrified and anxious, you reach down to lift, heal, and comfort us. Amen.

Monica Case Williams

God Has a Plan: Part I

"Take now thy son, thine only son Isaac, whom thou lovest, and get thee into the land of Moriah."

--Genesis 22:2

Have you ever wondered about the plans that God has for your life? We sometimes question the plans He has for us, because they may not make sense to us. When God told Abraham to take his only son to the land of Moriah and offer him for a burnt offering, it certainly did not make sense. Abraham might have questioned God's reasoning; nevertheless, he obeyed. God is in control, so we have to learn to trust Him. He will not lead us into blind alleys. He knows the plans He has for us. It might not seem logical; it might be a long and treacherous journey. To the human mind it might seem irrational, but God has a plan. It took Abraham three days to get to the appointed place which tells us that God is methodical. He takes His time, is never in a hurry, and is always on time.

"Take now thy son, thine only son Isaac, whom thou lovest."

Why would God give Abraham a promise then seemingly want to take it away? It was just a test because God had greater in store for him as he does for us. Despite your present circumstances, God will cause you to laugh again as He did with Sarah; God has not forgotten you. If He brings you what seems like an impossible situation, he can take you through.

Today, you might be in a place of weeping, but tomorrow, a place of joy. Abraham exercised his faith in God and God provided a ram. This was all part of God's plan. What doesn't make sense today could lead to your breakthrough tomorrow. Hold on, God's promises are sure.

Prayer

Lord, thank You for the plans you have for my life. I might not fully understand it now, but will as you unravel your secrets to me. Thank you for caring enough to make me a promise. Amen.

Beverly Coker

God Has a Plan: Part II

"Take now thy son, thine only son Isaac, whom thou lovest, and get thee unto the land of Moriah; and offer him there for a burnt offering upon one of the mountains which I will tell thee of."

--Genesis 22: 1,2

Many times, we question the circumstances of our lives because of things we do not understand. God sees the total picture, we see only a small portion of what He wants us to see. Job had a lot of questions for God, but God responded with questions that could only be answered by God. Why did God allow Job to suffer the loss of so many things? Job trusted God perhaps blindly, and even in his dark moments, his faith did not waver. Job must have realized that God had a plan.

Let's consider Abraham. He waited for the promised child, and when it seemed he was bonded to this child, God asked him to give him up. Certain things do not make sense, but God had a plan. This was a test of Abraham's faith.

Joseph, a young promising leader, went from the pit to the palace. Those were some of his worst days and yet some of his best days. But God had a plan. God's plan might cause you to suffer awhile but like Job "you shall come forth as gold" (Job 23:10).

Sarah was promised a son even in her old age. When she heard it, she laughed within herself. However, God caused her to laugh again because He had a plan. God's plan is always to bring you to a place of fulfilment, to unbelievable heights. Sometimes, His plan may not make sense. It might be long in coming and it might not look good on the surface, but He has a good plan.

God's plan for you might not happen as expected; neither will it come in the form you expected, but it will come.

"But as for you, ye thought evil against me, but God meant it unto good" (Genesis 50: 20).

"Weeping may endure for a night. but joy comes in the morning" (Psalm 30:5).

Your morning will come because God has a plan for you.

Prayer

Heavenly Father, help me to see the fulfilment of your plan for my life. Though it seems obscure from my vision, I know you are working it out. Help me to hold on and not to doubt. Amen.

Beverly Coker

Finding God in Difficult Times

"In the year that King Uzziah died I saw also the Lord sitting upon a throne, high and lifted up, and his train filled the temple."

--Isaiah 6:1

Have you ever felt overwhelmed by life? Have you ever had the experience when as one storm is winding down, another one is whipping up on the horizon? Life is full of challenges, but God is able to show himself mighty and strong even in the midst of the storms.

For Isaiah, the death of King Uzziah was not only a tragic national loss, it was a time of personal grief, seeing that the king was his cousin. Isaiah was experiencing the trauma of losing someone he admired and beloved.

When challenging situations come our way, whether through death, the loss of a significant relationship, sickness or financial hardship, we sometimes feel numb, angry, hurt, and confused. These are all normal feelings. How we respond to these feelings, can determine whether we remain in a perpetual cycle of sorrow.

One thing we see from Isaiah' example is that he went to the house of God. God expects us to come to him with everything. We are encouraged in the Word to cast all our cares upon the Lord (1 Peter 5:7).

Instead of spiraling out of control when trouble hit, Isaiah did something different – he went to the house of God and he saw the Lord. God is our very present help in trouble. He revealed himself to Isaiah at a very dark and vulnerable time in his life. Here in God's presence, Isaiah had a beautiful vision of the presence and glory of God.

His eyes were opened to see God's glory and his own humanity. As a result of this encounter, Isaiah received healing, cleansing, and commissioning, propelling him into his purpose as prescribed by God.

When we experience difficult situations in life, the best place to run is into the presence of our God.

Prayer

My Father, today I run to you, like a child running into the secure arms of a parent. I lay my cares at your feet and I pray that you will show up in all your glory to help me through this storm. In Jesus' name, Amen.

Rev. Michaelia Daubon

Our Encounter with Storms

"Master, careth thou not that we perish?"

--Mark 4: 38

Those of us who have experienced snow storms, hurricanes, and other types of storms know how devastating it can be. Storms have a way of showing up unexpectedly and often in the night time of our lives. Today, you might be in a storm, getting out of a storm or who knows, getting ready to face a storm. As long as you are in this life, you will encounter storms.

I would like to focus not just on physical storms, but on the storm of death, divorce, job loss, and other life events. Regardless of your relationship with God, you will face storms. In this scripture, Jesus wanted His disciples to go with Him to the other side, but first they had to go through a storm. These fishermen were experienced, yet they panicked when the boat began to fill with water.

Water might be in your boat today but let me assure you that you will not perish. When situations beyond our control confront us, we become fearful. These disciples cried out to Jesus, "Master, careth thou not that we perish?" In essence, they were accusing Jesus of neglecting them at a time when they needed Him the most. Jesus was asleep in the storm perhaps to test their faith. They knew Him, knew of His compassion, but in fear they wanted to be reminded that He cared.

Aren't you grateful that in moments of crisis Jesus still utters, "Peace be still?" In other words, this great wind must cease at His command, "Don't be afraid, I got it" he says. If you are experiencing fear today because water is in your boat, remember that Jesus is in the boat with you and

He won't let you drown.

Think of birds when there is a storm. They survive because they stay in the eye of the storm. That's where you and I need to be. In the eye, there is safety and protection. Psalm 34: "The eyes of the Lord are upon the righteous and His ears are open unto their cry." The Lord was not awakened by the wind nor the waves but by their cry.

Perhaps you need to be reminded that storms are temporary. So, hold on. This too will pass.

Prayer

Thank you for your covering and protection during the storms in my life. Teach me not to be afraid, but to trust you at all times. Amen.

Beverly Coker

God, Our Refuge

"God is our refuge and strength, an ever-present help in trouble."

--Psalm 46: 1 *NIV*

Refuge means a condition of being safe or sheltered from pursuit, danger, or trouble. It can also mean an institution providing accommodations for families who have suffered violence, or a disaster and needing help.

God is our refuge. He protects us in and through danger. No matter what we face, we know that as a Christian Christ stands on our behalf. Whenever we are attacked by the enemy, he pursues them until they are no more. He loves us with an everlasting love, that is why His blood means so much to us. So, as you go through difficult moments each day, remember that God will chase your enemy and bring comfort and hope to His children. I am not sure of the next move that God has for me or for you, but whether empty or full, we'll forever trust Him and continue to give Him the praise and worship that He deserves.

Sometimes, we stand, not because we have strength, but because God's eternal hand surrounds us and also the people that He places in our lives who help us along the way.

Sometimes, we walk not because we are powerful or strong but because His strength is made perfect in our weakness. That is why we are still standing. I thank Him for the many times that He sends help to me. Many times, those help was unexpected, but He is a God who works best when our strength is gone. There are times when a friend, a family member, or a co-worker would come to us and hold our hands and say, "You can make it."

So, whatever it takes, I will continue to look to God because He is the one who ultimately knows what we need, where we are, and how much we can bear. So today, we give all glory to God, Our Master, Our Savior and our Lord. We praise Him because He's the undefeated champion of love. Hallelujah.

The path that we take may be difficult, but let us be reminded that our Heavenly Father will take care of us.

Prayer

Lord, I call upon you today. I rest in you. I know that your protection is over me. Nothing will hurt me. I look to you. I trust in your love. And even when it seems like I will not make it, show me the way. I am willing to be led by you. No matter the circumstances, like Job, I commit to trust in you Lord. Guide me every day I pray. Amen.

Coleene Shaw

LOVE

The Love of God

"For God so Loved the World that He Gave…"

--John 3:16

It is difficult to comprehend the vastness and depth of God's love for us. Love is the very essence of God. Love is an emotion that each person needs in order to survive life's challenges/circumstances. Like the air we breathe, we need love to live. It is such an overwhelming, positive feeling to be the recipient of love and to give love in return.

There is a restorative quality to love. It restores health, relationships that have been severed, and gives new meaning to life. God demonstrated the greatest love by sending His own Son to die for mankind. You and I would not offer our child up for anyone. Yet God did it for us. It is amazing what people will do for the sake of love. As an outside observer, we might consider it to be crazy, but love defies rational thinking and takes things to the limit.

We are admonished to love others as we love ourselves (Mat 22:4). This is a tall order. If we did that, it would have a tremendous impact on our ability to forgive. We are inclined not to treat others kindly and not to overlook the faults and weaknesses of others. The Bible offers a radical approach to love by telling us to love those who spitefully use us, to love others as we love ourselves.

When we think of how amazing the love of God is and how He is willing to receive us into His merciful embrace despite our sinful nature, we should show that same love to others. God's love is a gift, an undeserved gift that we should be generous enough to extend to others.

God's love is transformative. It gives us a new perspective on life and encourages us to see each other through the light of Christ. There is a song that I love dearly: "The love of God is greater far than tongue or pen can ever tell." What an amazing love that is being extended to us today. Let us go forward and extend that love to someone who is undeserving of our love and especially of God's love.

Prayer

Father, thank you for your love to mankind. Teach us to love others as You have loved us. Let Your love shine through us today. Amen.

Beverly Coker

Love Thy Neighbor

"For in the resurrection they neither marry, nor are given in marriage, but are as the angels of God in Heaven."

--Matthew 22:30

"And the second is like, namely this. Thou shalt love thy neighbour as thyself. There is none other commandment greater than these."

--Mark 12: 31

It is common knowledge that while Jesus was on earth, He traveled extensively throughout Israel in various cities such as Galilee and Jerusalem. One day while on His journey, He came in contact with a teacher of the Law of Moses who overheard His conversation with a Sadducee about the woman who had married seven brothers. After their death and hers, Jesus was asked, "When God raises them from death, whose husband will she be?" Jesus answered, "They won't be married but rather they will be like angels in heaven." The Pharisees heard about the encounter and so they confronted Jesus. One among them was an expert in Jewish law. They questioned Jesus, "What is the most important commandment?" Jesus answered, "The most important one says: people of Israel, you have only one Lord and God, you must love Him with all your heart, soul, mind and strength."

Throughout the Gospel of Mark, much has been written about love. One of the most difficult requests made of humanity is probably that we love our neighbors just as much as we love ourselves. We all know how difficult people can be. However, I dare to challenge you, search yourself today. You may be surprised at what you find. Two friends who are neighbors no longer speak to each other because one made a trench in his backyard that leads water into his neighbor's property whenever it rains and causes soil erosion. After a heated argument about what should be done to alleviate the problem, the one getting the run-off threatened to shoot his neighbor. As Christians, we must be willing to listen, to understand, search for meaning, see Christ in others, and befriend our neighbors.

To those two neighbors, I would like to tell them that God loves both of them and has chosen them as His own special people. So be gentle, kind, humble, meek, and patient. Learn to tolerate each other and forgive each other. Remember one must forgive in order to be forgiven (See Colossians 3:12-15).

Prayer

God of Grace and Love, search me and know my heart today. Know where I fall short and teach me how to be a better person. In Christ's name I ask these things. Amen.

Percival Young

GRATITUDE

Gratitude

"Give thanks to the Lord, for he is good; his love endures forever."

--1 Chronicles 16:34

"Give thanks in all circumstances; for this is God's will for you in Christ Jesus."

--1 Thessalonians 5:1

It belongs to God, first and foremost! The bible says He inhabits our praises (Psalm 22:3). He likes it, He wants the recognition and the acknowledgement (not that He needs it) but, that His people may know that He is giver and creator of all things good.

How many of us would **cheerfully** continue to give (whatever it might be) to someone who receives and never says a 'thank you'? Ingratitude usually does not inspire joy. We teach our children to say, "Thanks" when something is given to them. Why? Because for one, it shows good manners, and two, appreciation to the giver. (Colossians 3:17).

While God loves our praises and receives them to Himself, at the same time, He is teaching us the importance of having an attitude of gratitude in living well, and in ever increasing good relationship with our fellowman, no matter what the circumstances might be. (1st Timothy 2:1-3); (Philippians 4:4-7).

***"IT IS A GOOD THING TO GIVE THANKS UNTO THE LORD"* (Psalm 92:1).**

Prayer:

Blessing, and glory, and wisdom, and thanksgiving, and honor, and power, and might, be unto our God for ever and ever. In the name of Jesus. **AMEN.**

Sonia Brown

Your Kindness Will Make Room for You

"And Jesse said unto David his son, Take now for thy brethren an ephah of this parched corn, and these ten loaves, and run to the camp to thy brethren."

--1 Samuel 17:17

Many times, when we read this passage about David and Goliath, our focus is on the victory of David. Today let's look at Jesse, David's father. In verse 17, we see where Jesse sent David to the camp to take food for his three brothers who were soldiers fighting in the war. When Jesse packed the food, he gave David more than enough to take for his brothers and he even placed in the package a good portion of cheese for the captain of the army. Oh, what generosity displayed! When Jesse did this, little did he know that his generosity was about to change his life.

In verse 25, the promise was given that the man who killed Goliath, the king would enrich him with great riches, and will give him his daughter in marriage and make his father's house free in Israel. Jesse was about to get his portion by getting a free house. He wouldn't have to pay taxes anymore.

If Jesse had not decided to send David to feed his brothers, this would not have happened. Luke 6:38 says, "Give and it will be given to you a good measure, pressed down, shaken together and running over, will be poured into your lap. For with the measure you use it will be measured to you." This is a good example of this scripture happening for Jesse – benefits extended to his household (or generations).

Prayer

That God will give us generous hearts which will make room for us. Amen.

Phenice McLean

The Lord's Supper

"For I have received of the Lord that which also I delivered unto you, That the Lord Jesus the same night in which he was betrayed took bread..."

-- Corinthians 11:23-26

Once a month, I am privileged to administer communion to the sick and shut-in. The Holy Communion is such a sacred experience. Communion is referred to in different ways: The Lord's Table, The Breaking of Bread (Acts 2:42). The purpose of communion is always forefront in my mind, which is to commemorate the death of Jesus Christ. The aim is to promote the communion of believers with Christ and the mutual communion of believers with each other.

The breaking of bread has been a practice since the Lord gave the commandment, and it's designed to stimulate in our hearts remembrance of the work of the cross. We are admonished to "do this in remembrance of Me" (1 Corinthians 11:25).

It is always such a solemn moment when we as brethren come together to celebrate and give thanks. The early church celebrated the death and resurrection of Jesus Christ by taking communion, sometimes every day (See Acts 2: 42-46). They saw it as an opportunity to recognize Jesus and thank God for what He has done. Lest we forget!! We must bear in mind that partaking of the Lord's Supper does not save or deliver us from sin. It is, in essence, a symbol of an inner work of faith. In other words, you ought to have had a relationship with Jesus before participating in the communion ceremony. To partake of the Lord's Table in an unworthy manner invites damnation to yourself. You need to give careful thought to what it signifies. The Lord's Supper is not just another meal. Examine yourself. Test your motives to be certain you are partaking for the right reason.

Communion reminds us of our need for on-going cleansing and renewal. It reminds us that "this is my body, which is broken for you" (1 Corinthians 11:23). "This cup is the new testament in my blood. This do ye as oft as ye drink it in remembrance of me" (verse 25). Lest we forget!!!

Today, let's give thanks for the work of the cross, for His body which was broken for us, and His blood which was shed for us.

Prayer

Thank you for bringing us redemption through Christ Jesus. By partaking of communion, we are celebrating you with thanksgiving in our hearts. Help us never to forget your love that was demonstrated on the cross. Amen.

Beverly Coker

A Grateful Heart

"Greater love has no one than this that, that a man lay down his life for his friends."

--John 15: 13

Today, I lift my heart in gratitude to God for His tremendous blessings upon my life. I am particularly grateful for faith, family, and friends.

Life without those three elements would be empty and meaningless. Gratitude is a deep expression of kindness received.

I am grateful for my faith in God. Without faith it would be impossible for me to please God. My faith in Him has empowered me, strengthened me, and given me hope at some of the lowest points in my life. I am thankful that early in my life, I discovered the benefits of following the Lord. Throughout my existence, I have experienced miracles, blessings in abundance, and God's guidance through my faith in him.

> *"The steadfast love of the Lord never ceases, His mercies never come to an end, they are new every morning, great is thy faithfulness."*

--Lamentation 3:22-24

Family: What can I say about family? I am from a large, close-knit family for whom I am truly grateful. In down times, they are my family; in high times they are my friends. I did not choose to be a member of this family; life made that selection. But every day, I give thanks for someone in my family: my siblings, husband, children and grand. What a blessed woman I am!

Finally, I give thanks for my friends. I place them in different categories, but they all come under the umbrella of friends. Some are closer in spirit than others, but I can always depend on someone to be a friend when I need one. Proverbs 18:24:

> *"A man that hath friends must shew himself friendly, and there is a friend that sticketh closer than a brother."*

I am not usually good at maintaining ongoing communication, yet even after months or sometimes years of not being in touch, we are able to resume our relationships without interruption. Proverbs 17:17 tells us "A friend loveth at all times." With increasing years, I have acquired a greater appreciation for people in general, especially for those whom I call family and friends.

I count my blessings every day and thank God for putting such wonderful people in my life. What a blessing!!!

Prayer

Heavenly Father, thank You for those who You have placed in my life. I am truly grateful. Amen.

Beverly Coker

Give Thanks with a Grateful Heart

"Oh, that men would praise the Lord for His goodness, and for his wonderful works to the children of men."

--Psalm 107:8

We thank God for the writers of the Psalms; they truly remind us of some of the things that we can and should give thanks for. I love to give thanks, because God has blessed me beyond my wildest imagination!

Based on that Psalm, my mind immediately went to the story that is told of the ten Lepers. Jesus could have said, "Ten lepers came to be healed. As they were on their way to show themselves to the Priest, they were all cleansed." He could have left the information there, but he proceeded to ask, "How many Lepers were cleansed?" Response – **Ten**. "How many came back to say thanks?" Response - **One**.

For the mere fact that Jesus makes reference to the one that came back to say thanks, it tells us that it matters to Him when we say thanks. We ourselves get upset and a little offended when we have extended ourselves to someone and they forget to say thanks. If I asked each person to share a time when he/she was offended by someone with an ungrateful heart, each would have a story of how it made them feel.

We thank God, first of all, for our salvation. *"Let the redeemed of the Lord say so, whom He has redeemed from the hand of the enemy"* (Psalm 107:2). We are reminded of the scripture that says, "No man can come to me, except the Father which hath sent me draw him" (John 6:7). Let us thank God for drawing us to Himself. There are many who are still groping in darkness, but He has snatched us from the hand of the enemy. Let us thank Him for our families, for our healing, our jobs, for covering us from near accidents, and the numerous blessings He has lavished upon us.

Let us try not to dwell on what the enemy is doing. God says he will fight with them that fight against us, and He will contend with them that contend with us. Our minds cannot conceive in a million years the things that God has done for us, seen and unseen.

"Oh, give thanks to the Lord, for He is good: for His mercies endureth forever" (Psalm 107:1).

Prayer

Father, we thank you for the many blessings you have given to us. Today we come to you with a grateful heart. Amen.

Paulette Joseph

FEAR

Overcoming Fear

"Fear not for I am with you."

--Isaiah 41: 1-10

We live in a world that is plagued with fear. Increasingly, as our world becomes more chaotic, even as Christians we grapple with intense fear. All of us experience fear. As humans, that is one of the emotions that we cannot escape. When we enter into any new situations, fear shows up, but we will never overcome if we give in to fear. I have had many fearful moments in my lifetime, but God always gives the courage to confront my fear.

Fear could rob you of a successful life, a blessed life. Always remember that "God has not given us a spirit of fear, but of power and of love and of a sound mind" (2 Tim. 1:7). Life is filled with many fearful situations. If left unchecked, it could rob you of peace, which is essential to navigate the complexities of life. Fear causes many people to become unproductive. They harbor inner fear that results in failure. It is estimated that the word "fear not" occurs in the Bible about 365 times. This means there is one for each day. So why are we so fearful when the Bible says, "Fear not?"

"Whenever I am afraid, I will trust in you" (Psalm 56:3).

Fear can be devastating. It can master us, frighten us, destroy us, and that is why we need the supernatural power of God to conquer the effects of fear. Faith in God is essential if we are to overcome our fears. God gives us courage to live our lives as He intended. Fear should not be a handicap to our success. Let us go forward with boldness, knowing that the Bible tells us repeatedly, "Fear not." (Isaiah 41:10) "Fear not for I am with you."

Prayer

Father, teach me to trust you and not to be afraid. I thank you that your presence in me is able to conquer my fears. Amen.

Beverly Coker

God's Promise

"Yea, though I walk through the valley of the shadow of death, I will fear no evil for thou art with me."

--Psalm 23:4

I can see that the times when I feared the task before me was too difficult to manage, The Lord made a way. One of my earliest memories was a fear of being alone in my own home in England while my husband (of one year) flew missions somewhere in Europe. I had no prior fear, but that day, I just could not stay in my own home alone. I called a friend, another U.S. military wife, and expressed my fear. She said, "Come on over. You can stay here with my family." So, I went to her home and after a cup of tea and about a half hour of visiting, the Holy Spirit spoke quietly to me: "Yea, though I walk through the valley of the shadow of death, I will **fear no evil** for **thou art with me**" (V. 4).

After hearing this well-known scripture within me, I said to my friend, "I can go home now." She asked with curiosity, what was different now than it was half an hour ago? I was able to say with confidence that I had a promise from our God (a Rhema Word) and I had no reason to fear because He was with me. That scripture was one I had learned while a child in Sunday School.

Another lesson learned from that experience was to ensure that, when my husband and I had children, I would ensure that they would have early biblical training so that they would be able to stand against the giants of fear and doubt that they would experience.

Prayer

Dear God, thank you for Your promises. Help me to always remember them.

Diane Crosley-Mayers

Walking in the Valley of the Shadow

"Yea, though I walk through the valley of the shadow of death, I will fear no evil: for thou art with me; thy rod and thy staff they comfort me."

--Psalm 23:4 *KJV*

The sad news shattered my world. Shena, my brother's daughter, had taken ill again. Her cancer had returned with an unstoppable, unimaginable fury, and the entire family was devastated.

Shena is a young and vibrant forty- something year old wife and mother whose articles of hope and encouragement have appeared in her church magazine. Shena's pretty face has been seen almost weekly on social media giving praise to God for his miraculous healing of her body from the greedy grasp of cancer.

Her testimony was that she had been healed, and her determination and resolve were seen in her changed diet and the herbs she ingested daily to maintain her healing. On Facebook, she could be seen exercising on a treadmill, sweating furiously with a broad smile on her face. Her messages always (without fail) spoke of God's goodness. In my mind, I saw her as God's cheerleader, one who challenged all of us who were "going through" to trust Him despite how grim things appeared.

But now, just hours ago, the sad news came that the cancer has metastasized and that she has been placed in hospice. It is especially poignant to me, a cancer survivor of four years, for I have held onto Shena's words of optimism with great hope in the face of my fear and sometimes shaky faith.

Each of us has a moment when we come face – to – face with fearful situations that could create a crisis of faith. Will we believe God when the outcomes we hope for and God's ultimate will for our lives don't align? We know that God, Who has all power, can with a word, reverse any dire situation whether it is medical, emotional, marital, financial, or legal. My prayer is when those times come, and they must certainly will, that we never doubt God's great power and love for us. Whatever we encounter, He is with us.

Prayer

Father, in your most precious name, I come to you thanking you for the examples and guideposts you put in our lives who give us wise counsel and illuminate our path. Help us to trust you in every situation. In Your name, I pray. Amen.

Rev. Clara Ruffin

Be Not Afraid

"The Lord is my light and my salvation; whom shall I fear? The Lord is the strength of my life; of whom shall I be afraid."

--Psalm 27:1

When my Mom was in her mid-nineties and needed twenty-four-hour nursing care, with love in our hearts for her best interest and in consultation with the medical staff, the family decided that she would best be served by moving her into a nursing facility.

Mother was in the early stages of dementia. She also had some vision and hearing loss so her ability to read her Bible daily was limited, but her long-term memory was fantastic.

One Sunday when I visited the facility where my mom was, one of her caregivers asked to speak with me. To my surprise, she wanted to know what the "Psalms" were.

My mother in her confinement in a nursing facility was ministering to the staff using the Psalms which she had memorized from her youth. She recited the Psalms which she called upon each and every day of her life for strength and guidance.

The young caregiver had never heard of the Psalms before my mother started to recite them to her every Sunday morning and she was intrigued. She wanted to know where to find the Psalms and especially the one that talked about light and salvation, which Mother recited often. This encounter was truly transformative for the young caregiver. God uses us in many ways to share His message of love and salvation. Sometimes, we are unaware of how God calls us to be disciples, but He equips us when we are called to do His work. (See Psalm 27: 1-14).

This Psalm shows the Psalmist's belief in the mighty power and the greatness of God.

> *"The lord is the stronghold of my life, of whom shall I be afraid?"* (verse 1).

As Christians, we need to be grounded in the knowledge that there is a power far greater than ours or any that we can imagine. Psalm 27 is relevant in our world today as we seek to be sheltered from the evil and the violence in society.

> *"Though a host encamp against me, my heart shall not fear, though war rise against me, yet I will be confident."* (verse 3).

We need to be confident that the Heavenly light will brighten our path every turn we take, every move we make, as long as we trust God and believe His promises.

Prayer

We give thanks, oh God, for the messages of the Psalms. May they continue to inspire our hearts and bring comfort and peace to a world that has turned upside down. Amen.

Nora M. Brown

Do Not Worry

"With men this is impossible; but with God all things are possible."

--Matthew 19:26

No one knows my story. I worry about tomorrow, although I know it will take care of itself. As I get older and realize that my time here is shorter, I can't help but wonder if I am doing my all to please God.

My struggles with worry are not solved by answers or quick remedies. Daily, I seek answers from the Bible to help me grow beyond worries into a trusting relationship with God. Nothing happens in this world that is beyond the knowledge or power of our God. He is everywhere! (Psalm139:7-12). He knows everything. I don't know my future, but God does, and He knows my every need (Psalm 33:13-14). God is all powerful. He has limitless power and His own reason for what He permits (Matt. 19:26). God, I believe is more concerned about my health, my work, my friends, family, and daily well-being.

I know worry is an expression of my fears of the future. Fear has been around, I believe, since Adam and Eve hid from God among the trees and covered themselves with leaves. Knowing and understanding that God is a good God drives my fears away, even when I know that I have sinned.

In a broken world, and our short comings, we have no guarantees except that God can be trusted. He will never leave not forsake us.

> *"Fear not for I am with you.. Be not dismayed, for I am your God."* (Isaiah 41:10).

Worry can either bring us to the Father in Heaven, or it will drive us away from Him.

Over the years, I have the support of a prayer partner. That relationship has drawn me closer to God and I am less fearful of tomorrow. When I worry, I turn my attention to my God. I remind myself that He is in charge. He can carry our burdens and take away my fears. He sustains me and He will never leave me. No one knows my story, but daily I am learning to turn my worry into prayer.

My daily prayer is acknowledging that this is the day that the Lord has made, I will rejoice in it. I ask God to help me each day to live life to the fullest, as I know tomorrow is not promised.

Prayer

Heavenly Father, help me to trust You at all times and not to worry. I know You are in charge, so teach me not to worry about tomorrow. Amen.

Ursula Brown

Fear

"The Lord is my Light and my salvation, whom shall I fear? The Lord is the strength of my life, of whom shall I be afraid?"

--Psalm 27:1

We see from these two verses that David had some temptation of fear coming towards him. He had to remind himself who God was to him: his Light, his Salvation and the strength of his life. The scripture reminds us that of the characters we read about in the Bible, David, Moses, Elijah to name a few, we are all of like passions. We face counter attacks to God's truth every day. As David did, we have to decree and declare in the atmosphere that fear is not of God. I don't think David whispered these words but spoke with confidence.

Psalm 111:10 reminds us that the fear of the Lord is the beginning of wisdom. Godly fear gives us confidence. He knows the challenges that we face, particularly with our families, our children, marriage, on the job, health issues, to name a few. We have the assurance in **2 Timothy 1:7** that God has not given us the spirit of fear, but of power, love, and a sound mind.

Matthew 8:23 reminds us to remind ourselves of the story of Jesus, when he was asleep in a ship, and the waves became boisterous. His disciples awoke him and said, "Lord save us, we perish!" Jesus said to them as he is saying to us, "Why are you fearful, O ye of little faith?"

The winds do become very boisterous and at times last for a long season, but God admonishes us today, "Trust me." He has the power to rebuke the winds and the waves, and no weapon that is formed against us will prosper. We must also remind ourselves that not everything that happens to us is from the enemy. God uses circumstances to test us. Have you ever heard the saying, "Our trials come to make us stronger?" They do. We must agree that when we have overcome our trials with God's help, our faith level is lifted higher, and our testimonies help other believers to encourage them that they will overcome too.

Job 39 reminds us how awesome and powerful our God is. In **Job 40:10**, as God encouraged Job, He further encourages us, "Deck yourself with majesty and excellency; and array thyself with glory and beauty!" Let us put on the garment of Praise, for any spirit of heaviness! The God of Hosts is with us; the God of Jacob is our refuge! If God be for us, who can stand against us? The response is a resounding, "No one!!"

Prayer

Heavenly Father, as we put our confidence in You, we need not fear any evil. We thank You for the assurance of Your presence with us and that knowledge dispels our fear. Amen.

Paulette Joseph

Fear Not

"What time I am afraid, I will trust in thee."

--Psalm 56: 3

"Fear not; for I am with thee; be not dismayed; for I am thy God: I will strengthen thee; yea, I will help thee; yea I will uphold thee with the right hand of my righteousness."

--Isaiah 41:10

How many times have we read the words "Fear Not" in the Bible? Most of us would say many times. Well it has been reported that the words "Fear Not" have been recorded 365 times in the Bible. It is believed to be the most frequent command in the Bible. Is this a coincidence we might ask? Why 365 times? The conclusion is since there are 365 days in the year, the Omniscient God knew we would become fearful on a daily basis. Therefore, it is His daily reminder to us to live each day without fear.

Is this an easy task? Not at all. We all can attest to the fact that we are subject to fear in all areas of our lives. It could be spiritually, physically, emotionally, financially, or otherwise. What then is the solution? Just stick to the Word of God. My suggestion is that we make a list of some of the Bible passages that encourage us "Not to be afraid" and memorize them. Whenever the situation arises that we need them, we naturally would turn to them and the God of Peace will comfort and give His peace.

Psalm 56 is a very comforting Psalm. Read it through and highlight (verse 3) which says, "What time I am afraid I will trust in thee." This speaks of total confidence in God as we trust in Him. Most of us have our scripture passages that we quote and embrace in times of need. This is a good thing. It makes our faith grow stronger. One of my favorites is Isaiah 41:10, "Fear thou not for I am with thee… yea I will uphold thee with the right hand of my righteousness." May you be blessed as you read and meditate on this verse.

Prayer

Dear Lord, You are the Omnipresent God. Thank You that You are always with us. Help us to dwell on this always. We bless your Name that because You live, we can face tomorrow and because You live all fear is gone. Amen.

GAT

Who Walks in the Valley?

"Yea, though I walk through the valley of the shadow of death, I will fear no evil: for thou art with me; thy rod and thy staff they comfort me."

--Psalm 23:4

In the book of Psalms, there is a famous passage in Chapter 23 known as "the 23rd Psalm" that we teach our children and we pray quite often. Verse 4 is our focus today. It says:

> *"Yea, though* ***I*** *walk through the valley of the shadow of death,* ***I*** *will fear no evil: for thou art with me; thy rod and staff they* ***comfort*** *me."*

Who is the "I" in this verse referring to? Did you know that it is you and I? This is a personal encounter that no one escapes. All of us are to identify with this "I" because we all will at some point walk through the valley.

The valley is a place that could make you filled with fear while going through it, but there is a rod and staff present to bring you comfort. So, no matter who you are, you will walk in the valley, but rest assured it's a meeting place between you and God. We must and will go through that valley, maybe one time or many times on different occasions and circumstances. But remember, the Savior is always present in the valley. Who goes through the valley? It is you and I along with the Savior.

Prayer

Remind me, Lord, that you are there with us going through the valley. Amen.

Phenice McLean

PRAISE AND THANKSGIVING

Let Us Give Thanks

"It is a good thing to give thanks unto the Lord, and to sing praises unto Thy name, O Most High."

--Psalm 92:1

Once a year, this great nation pauses to celebrate a day set aside to offer thanks to God for His bountiful blessings to us as a nation. We call it "Thanksgiving Day." To those of us who have been favored with daily blessings, we should make this a regular part of our daily activities. The Psalm reminds us, "It is a good thing to give thanks unto the Lord and to sing praises unto Thy name" (Psalm 92:1).

We sometimes give thanks for a particular event in our lives, like the birth of a child, getting a new job, a house, a promotion, the list goes on. Do we take time to thank Him for His daily favors, favors that we cannot repay and for which we do not deserve? Lamentations so beautifully states, "Great is thy faithfulness" (Lamentations 3:23). Morning by morning new mercies we see.

As we find ourselves busily preparing for the holiday season, let us begin by thanking God for extending His love towards us by sending His Son to die for us. Having received that gift, let us extend our love to the worthy and the unworthy. So often, we are dismayed about the issues that confront this nation and in fact, the whole world. The songwriter reminds us that "love is the remedy." It is impossible to itemize the things for which we should be grateful. However, the God of mercy and grace truly sees the sincerity of our hearts when we pause just to say, "Thank You."

"O give thanks unto the Lord, call upon His name: make known His deeds among the people" (Psalm 105:1).

Prayer

Dear Father, for your blessings to us each day, especially for life, make us truly grateful. Amen.

Beverly Coker

Living in the Light

"But you are a chosen generation, a royal priesthood, a holy nation, a peculiar people, that he should shew forth the praises of Him who hath called you out of darkness into His marvelous light."

--1 Peter 2:9

Our eyes were designed to adjust to the light and the darkness. Anyone who has spent a long period of time in darkness will find that patience is necessary when coming into the light. We get so excited about the light that we forget our eyes need time to adjust so we can see clearly.

Since our eyes have learned to focus in darkness, it creates a problem for the person coming out of darkness. It's here where we are confronted to make a choice: facing the light or returning to the darkness. The darkness has been comfortable and familiar to you. The dark is filled with ignorance, wickedness, and lies. The light is filled with awareness, wisdom and truth. We have to make a choice. Either we choose to stay in the dark and remain comfortable or seek truth and discover what greatness lies in the light.

It's a scary thing to face the truth when you've been influenced by a life in the darkness. Living in the light will change your thoughts, relationships, and beliefs, which is very necessary. Jesus is the light; in Him there is no darkness. We move to another dimension when we live in the light. Light dispels darkness, as we dwell in that light, we reflect the glory of God.

Prayer

Father, I thank You that You are the light that lightens our darkness. Help us to walk continuously in the light. Amen.

Pastor Stonewall Hunter

Be Thankful and Grateful

"For I have learned, in whatsoever state I am, therewith to be content."

--Philippians 4:11

A man had twin sons. One seemed to be always wanting more and the other seemed content with whatever came his way. The father decided to put them to be ultimate test.

On their birthday when they were at school, he placed several electronic toys and gadgets in the room of the son who never seemed contented, and in the room of the other he placed a load of horse manure. Upon their return from school, he gave them time alone in their room and then he visited. He found the son to whom he had given toys, with his hands folded and a sneer on his face, saying, "You have given me all these toys and gadgets but what am I going to do when the batteries die?" He visited the son in the room filled with horse manure and found him stirring the pile of horse manure. With a smile he said, "Dad there must be a pony somewhere in this pile."

Paul said in the reading of Philippians 4: 12-13 that he had learned to be satisfied in whatever circumstances he found himself. He expressed gratitude and thankfulness that God has provided for us as He sees our needs. His Word promises that if we trust Him, He will supply all our needs.

Because we have trust in Him, we have hope that beyond the present, the future is secure, and we wait in anticipation for what He has in store for us. We need not worry or moan or fret because He is our God. Trust in God fills us with optimism in our outlook instead of being pessimistic. If the battery runs out, He will provide more. Where there is horse manure, there is a horse.

Prayer

Heavenly Father make us truly grateful for giving us hope and a future. Amen.

JAT

Fearfully and Wonderfully Made

"I will praise You, for I am fearfully and wonderfully mad; Marvelous are Your works, and that my soul knows very well."

--Psalm 139: 14 *NKJV*

So many people live their lives not knowing why they are on earth. Each person has a divine destiny. Every human being has pondered his or her own mortality. We have asked ourselves questions about our origin and are obsessed with our future. Specifically, we want to answer this question, "Why am I here?"

When we ponder the origin of mankind and contemplate the depths of our destiny, we often situate our thoughts around the notion that there is a higher power that is in control of our lives. Our past is history, today is our present, but the future remains a mystery.

David, the Patriarch, surveyed his own mortality and emphatically stated, "I am fearfully and wonderfully made. Marvelous are thy works and that my soul knoweth well" (Psalm 139:14).

Man's chief aim is to glorify God. We are born to worship and serve God (Revelation 4:11. Saint Augustine, the great theologian said, "Thou hast made us for thyself, O Lord, and our heart is restless until it finds its rest in thee" (Augustine of Hippo, Confessions).

That there exists an insatiable appetite for satisfaction that is resident in each of us is an indisputable fact. However, true satisfaction and happiness seem to be elusive. I like to say, that there is a hole in our soul. Some people try to fill this void in their soul by using deleterious substitutes such as drugs, alcohol, illicit sex, and the list goes on.

When we realize that we are "Fearfully and wonderfully made" for a divine purpose, life becomes more meaningful. We will ardently cultivate the most important relationship…our relationship with our creator, God. Moreover, we will respect ourselves and others; we become selfless and caring, rather than selfish and careless. We will live as we were created, like one who is a unique masterpiece…impossible to be duplicated and essentially, one who is "…fearfully and wonderfully made."

Prayer

Creator God, I acknowledge that you made me to be a unique person. I submit to your purpose for my life. Please help me to walk in the path of righteousness. Help me to honor you with my life as I walk toward fulfilling my destiny. Thank You, Sovereign Lord, for hearing my prayer. Amen!

Byron G.E. Peart, D.Min.

Giving Praise to God

"I will bless the Lord at all times; His praise shall continually be in my mouth."

--Psalm 34:1

Praising God is part of our created purpose. However, praise comes naturally for us when life is at its best and everything is working in our favor. Praise doesn't seem to flow as freely when life takes a difficult turn. It may be a foreclosure, a bad diagnosis from the doctor, or the loss of a loved one. Are we able to praise God then? This is a question that is presented to every believer. Job faced this same question and his response is a model for the believer. He said, "The Lord gave, and the Lord has taken away; "Blessed be the name of the Lord." (Job 1:21)

Seven years ago, when the Doctor told me that my husband of 25 years was dead, I was also faced with the same question: "Am I able to praise God now?" It was the hardest season of my life and though my tears flowed, praise, echoed through my tears and is still echoing today. "I will bless the Lord at all times." God is faithful, He comforts, He Heals, He provides and He is a Promise Keeper.

Prayer

Dear God, we thank You for Your faithfulness. Please give us the grace to praise You at all times. Help us to remember that "you will never leave us nor forsake us." Amen.

Rev. Pearl Huggins

It's All Good

"For I know the thoughts that I think toward you, saith the Lord, thoughts of peace, and not of evil, to give you an expected end."

--Jeremiah 29:11

Praise and gratitude really do move the hand and heart of a person. Standing in the kitchen, prepping breakfast, and thinking about what I'm going to prepare for another event, I started to smile at the memory of meals I have prepared that my family and friends have enjoyed and in essence praised.

In that moment, I literally felt the joy of the Holy Spirit connecting my thoughts to how our Father feels when we praise him and reminisce on the good things He does in our daily lives. The praise and gratitude of my family and friends really move my heart to think of something more scrumptious to make.

I believe that's how our Father feels. I envision Him smiling, rubbing his hands together and thinking of ways to TOP his last good work in your life and mine. What a wonderful God we serve! Whose ways, thoughts and heart towards us are only good!

"I alone know the plans I have for you, plans to bring you prosperity and not disaster, plans to bring about the future you hope for" (Jeremiah 29:11).

Prayer

Dear Father, I am grateful to You for Your blessings towards me. I praise You for the blessings You have bestowed upon me. For that I am truly grateful. Amen.

Rev Alicia Morgan

Alleluia, Alleluia, Alleluia

"And after these things I heard a great voice of much people in heaven, saying, Alleluia; Salvation, and glory, and honour, and power, unto the Lord our God."

--Revelation 19: 1

At church, during praise and worship, we sing Alleluia to Jesus our King. When we do so, it's from hearts of thanksgiving and praise. There is a song we love to sing that says, "My Alleluia belongs to You," referring to Jesus. There is no one on earth who is more uplifted than when we offer praises to Almighty God and to Jesus. What is great to know is that this song will not only be sung on earth, but also by the saints in heaven. In Revelation 19:1, we see where the people in heaven are saying, "Alleluia, Salvation, and glory, honor, and power belong to the Lord our God."

I am excited to report to you that praise and worship is not just for time but also for eternity. Let us continue to rehearse and practice to shout those Alleluias every chance we get because it will be ours in eternity. Verse 6 says, "And I heard as it were the voice of a great multitude." Just imagine a great multitude of believers with different tongues, languages, and speech saying the same word, "Alleluia" over and over again! Let us continue to rehearse for the real occasion in eternity. When is this going to happen? Verse 7 says when the marriage of the Lamb is come.

Be blessed and say your "Alleluias," not only in church, but every opportunity that you may get.

Prayer

Let us pray today that we will ever lift up praises to the Most High God and King. Amen.

Phenice McLean

Thankful to God

"Oh, that men would praise the Lord for his goodness, and for his wonderful works to the children of men!"

--Psalm 107:31

Practice thanking God daily. Thankfulness lifts you up above your circumstances. We all have sinned and deserve God's judgment, but He sent His only Son to satisfy that judgment. He loved us so much He died for our sins.

We should give thanks because His faithfulness, grace, and mercy endure for all generations. Be thankful for the material and spiritual blessings that He gives to us. We seem dissatisfied with what we have and the situation that we are in.

Rich or poor, healthy or sick, we should not forget how dependent we are on God for everything. Let us thank God for the good things and the not so pleasant things. Thank Him for everything that comes our way. We should not let a day go by without thanking Him for His mercy and His grace to us.

Prayer

God, please help me to have a heart of thanksgiving and to thank you daily for your grace and mercy. Father, all I have needed you have provided, and I am forever thankful. Help me to bring glory for your many blessings. Amen.

Hannah Fevrier

Praise: The Unused Weapon

"Offer unto God thanksgiving; and pay thy vows unto the most High."

--Psalms 50:14

We are instructed in the scripture to worship the Lord with praise and thanksgiving. We are to give God the glory that is due unto His Holy Name. I have learned firsthand how important it is to worship God. A few years ago, I remember waking up one morning and falling down on my knees to pray. During this time, the Holy Spirit began to speak to me, and He simply instructed me not to ask Him for anything but instead just to give Him praise. At that very moment, I began to give Him praise and worship. Throughout the rest of the day, the Holy Spirit continued to instruct me to just praise Him whenever I prayed. I remained in obedience. I could not understand why the Holy Spirit continuously instructed me to just praise. However, you know how the saying goes, "When the praises go up, then the blessings come down."

On this day, unbeknownst to me, my sister had been traveling on the back of a pickup truck. When she had reached a part of the journey, the driver looked back and decided to ask a young man who was driving in the passenger side to trade places with her. He decided to do this simply because he did not like the idea of seeing a young lady driving on the back of the truck. After trading places, they continued on their journey and unfortunately met in a car accident. The young man who had so graciously traded place with my sister was badly hurt and died on the scene. Wow… although this was a very unfortunate incident, it is my belief because of my obedience to the Holy Spirit, my sister's life was spared. The praises went up even before I knew what I was praising Him for. The blessing came down after giving God praise throughout the entire day.

Sometimes when we enter into God's magnificent presence, we list all of the things we desire, but it is so important to start our time with Him in a mode of praise and worship—He is too good to us. The Word of God reminds us that God does not eat the flesh of animals but instead He inhabits the praises of His people. Let us exalt Him in worship and give Him the glory that is due to His name.

Praise sets the stage for us to ask God anything.

In Psalm 50:14-15, it states that, after offering God thanksgiving, we are then invited to ask anything of Him. After thanking Him, we will be able to call upon Him in the days of trouble and He promises to rescue us.

Prayer

Father, I thank you that I can approach You with thanksgiving in my heart. I want to thank you for things seen and unseen. For blessings of yesterday and tomorrow. Amen.

Rev. Elaine Beckford

TRIALS/SUFFERING

Mourn with Those Who Mourn

"...the Father of mercies, and the God of all comfort."

--1 Corinthians 1:3

Each new day, I thank God for the gift of life. We often take life for granted until we are impacted by the loss of a loved one. As a minister, I am blessed to be a comforter. Each time a homicide occurs in my city, I am notified and along with a group of Chaplains, we visit the family of the victim. Too often, young lives are snuffed out by the senseless actions of others.

Today, I made arrangements to visit with the mother of a 17-year-old who was killed through violence. What can we say to a grieving mother at such a time as this? An important person in her life has been taken away prematurely. We can only turn to "the God of all comfort: who comforteth us in all our tribulations" (1 Corinthians 1:3). We are able to endure the darkest moments of our lives through the help of God. We are conquerors, not after our suffering, but even in our suffering.

Death comes to each of us at one time or the other. Paul says, "For me to live is Christ and to die is gain" (Phi. 1:20). Not many of us relish the thought of death, but those of us who know Christ can go forward with hope. *"If in this life we have hope in Christ, we are of all men most miserable"* (1 Corinthians 15: 19).

Death is a transition to a place prepared for us, so we need not fear death but embrace it. Death often causes brokenness. But God brings beauty out of brokenness and provides comfort through the Christian community. Brokenness doesn't imply that you are weak or lack faith. Instead, it's a human condition that relieves us of pain and heartache. I often encourage those experiencing the loss of a loved one to weep if necessary. It's a catharsis that heals. *"Weeping may endure for a night but joy cometh in the morning"* (Psalm 30:5). Mourning doesn't last forever. How long an individual mourns depends on his/her relationship with the deceased. Morning comes at some point and it brings joy in reflecting on the life of the departed. As Christians, we grieve with hope.

Prayer

Heavenly Father, thank you for the comfort that you give especially in times of sorrow. May you bring comfort to broken hearts today. Amen.

Beverly Coker

The Fight

"For by thee I have run through a troop: by my God have I leaped over a wall. As for God, his way is perfect; the word of the Lord is tried: he is buckler to all them that trust in him."

--2 Samuel 22:30-31

It is near impossible to live or walk through this life without facing difficult circumstances. One is probably coming to mind right now. The one or many, fraying your patience, your fortitude, or your personal reserve. I call them, those 'common to man' moments. The Lord gave me this image of a boxing match. You, the contender, at a boxing match, you did not schedule, expect, or feel prepared for. But, somehow, life circumstances have called you to the center of the ring, to square off with the opponent, aka the 'common to man'. The invisible bell dings, signaling it's on and ready or not, that 'common man' has his dukes up, ready to rumble.

Can you picture it? Have you been there? Are you in the thick of a fight right now? It can feel like an isolating experience. However, I want you to read just the bifocals of your imagination. I want you to renew your mind to the rules of the game, because the boxing match you are imagining is not similar to the one I pictured. In my image, the "common man" is scheduled for defeat.

John 16 spotlights you, the Contender, the one standing in the gap, declaring victory over your life, your marriage, your children, your home, your finances, your dream, your purpose, or to whatever it is you are commanding to be at peace. In John 16, Jesus has spent a whole chapter giving the disciples the playbook on the opponent. He says, the opponent is going to throw the book at you. He's going to give you all the trouble he can, but know this, your opponent has lost. No matter the form, he assumes in your life, he stands judged and condemned.

To you, however, He says, "I tell you this, so that you will be at peace. Yes, you are going to face a lot of trouble, it's inevitable, but know this, take heart, I have overcome the world" (See John 16:33). In essence, so will you. It's in the affirmative. Be ever so still. Find that place of peace. Know that you are slated to overcome. The issues in your life have already been judged and found to be illegal, a below the belt hit, that's deemed an automatic foul.

Prayer

For by You I can run upon a troop;

By my God I can leap over a wall.
As for God, His way is blameless;
The word of the Lord is tested;
He is a shield to all who take refuge in Him.

Amen.

Minister Alicia Morgan

What Do You Do When the Hurt Does Not Heal?

"And the Lord said unto Satan, hast thou considered my servant Job, that there is none like him in the earth, a perfect and an upright man, one that feareth God, and escheweth evil? And still he holdeth fast his integrity, although thou movedst me against him, to destroy him without cause."

--Job 2:3

There are some experiences that are common to all of us regardless of race, sex, class, age, personality, or situation. Chief among these is the experience of happiness and the experience of hurt.

Most of us find that happiness and hurt are woven together in this patchwork called life. There are times when one or the other seems to rule our lives. However, when the situation is reversed and the pain of life blots out all that was once good in our lives, we are put to life's most crucial test.

It is a fact that hurt hurts, whether it is self-inflicted – as it sometimes is – or hurt inflicted by other people, or systems, or structures of power. The bottom line is....hurt hurts!

As we ponder the condition of human hurt, there is challenge and prescription in the story of the servant of God, Job who was the leading citizen in the community of Uz. Job was blessed beyond measure; he held the unique distinction of being bragged about by God. Job enjoyed the love of his family and the respect of his neighbors.

Then, something happened. God, in His sovereignty allows things to happen that are inexplicable to man. The trouble began with a conversation between God and Satan. Job was completely unaware of this conversation as he continued with his daily affairs. Then, suddenly, without warning, the most blessed citizen of Uz became the most wretched. Now, he may have been able to give up cattle and oxen and sheep; but there are very few of us who could remain standing after hearing the news that we had lost all our children. Stripped of possessions and family, he was left with one wife, four servants, and great grief. In all this, Job remained faithful to God; he prevailed over Satan's destructive plans and God restored him (See Job 42:12).

What do we do when the hurts do not heal?

Look to Jesus who was wounded for our transgressions, bruised for our iniquities. Look to Him who has deliverance in His step, healing in His touch, life in His voice, hope in His hand, love in His heart, our living in His dying. Look at Him – healing crippled lives as well as crippled limbs, healing our hurts, forgiving our sins. Look to Him! Amen.

Prayer

Gracious Lord, we look to You when we are in the midst of the struggle and pain of life. We look to You, our strength and our redeemer. In the name of Jesus! Amen.

Rev. Tracy Johnson Russell, Rector

Coping with Hard Times

"And the peace of God which passeth all understanding shall keep your hearts and minds through Christ Jesus."

--Philippians 4:7

We all face situations that are overwhelming and perplexing which lead us to wonder, "Does anyone care?" "Does Jesus care?" Everyone battles through hardship, but as Christians, we have hope and ways of coping. Paul admonishes us to turn these situations over to God through prayer, knowing that God always has a way of escape. Don't give in. Don't give up. Instead, look to the hills from whence cometh your help.

Again, Paul tells us to "Be careful for nothing but in everything by prayer and supplication with thanksgiving let your request be made known unto God" (Philippians 4:6). God still specializes in miracles. He knows how to level mountains and calm troubled seas. There is nothing that you face that is beyond the reach of God's mercy.

James reminds us to "consider it joy" (1: 2). How can we be joyful when we are being tested and life's trials cause us to question our very existence? No matter what your circumstances may be, you can find joy in the presence of God. Joy is attainable through God. Rejoice in the fact that God understands you well and knows exactly what you are experiencing. God permits us to experience hardship to bring us into a deeper and more intimate relationship with Him. The songwriter states, "Through it all I've learned to trust in Jesus, I've learned to depend on Him."

The end result of our dependence on God is peace. God's peace transcends our human conditions and gives us strength to face our challenging situations. We can flourish in the face of hardship because of the power of God at work within us.

Prayer

Father, thank you for peace that allows me to face every difficult circumstance. You are my strong tower. Amen.

Beverly Coker

It's Just a Test

"My brethren, count it all joy when ye fall into divers temptations; knowing this, that the trying of your faith worketh patience."

--James 1:2 & 3

Have you ever been watching TV and was startled by a loud news flash that says, "This is just a test?" Whatever problem you might be facing today, it's just a test to reveal your true character. God might be permitting the enemy to test you in order to see how much you can withstand. Many of us go through the refiner's fire, the process through which gold is refined. God wants to make us into better or more polished human beings, but we must go through some degree of testing. It's often in such times that we learn to lean on Him, trust Him, and prove His love for us. I think of Elijah (1 King 17) and his encounter with the widow and her son. He requested of her all that she had to maintain life for herself and her son. Reluctantly, she yielded to his request and by faith gave the little she had. Little did she know that this was just a test because ultimately, she gained much more than she had given. God sometimes interrupts our life with situations that require our complete dependence on him. This too might be just a test.

James reminds us that the trying of our faith worketh patience (1: 3); it makes us into better people. Therefore, we should count it all joy. We are all faced with tests whether health, relationships, social or spiritual, but rejoice, that we can come forth as pure gold.

Testing is similar to a tree being pruned, but ultimately it yields precious fruit and becomes a better tree for having gone through that process.

Rejoice that your trials are only temporary and are just a test.

"Whom the Lord loveth he chasteneth" (Hebrews 12:6).

Prayer

Lord, I know that you are with me even in my times of testing. I pray that you will help me to become a better person. Amen.

Beverly Coker

Understanding the Shadow!

"Yea, though I walk through the valley of the shadow of death, I will fear no evil: for thou art with me; thy rod and thy staff they comfort me."

--Psalm 23:4 *KJV*

The real thing was not there. It was only a shadow. It was only after I'd walked through the dark place in my life that the healing began. Yet, there was something that kept trying to torment me, lurking in the shadow.

I realized God had begun to heal me, but the shadow didn't want to give up. It kept presenting itself, trying to hold me in the painful place. The more I cried out to God, the less the shadow was present. It began to diminish, not being as bright and strong as it was in the beginning.

Today, I stand, sit, walk, and live in the confidence that God is bringing me through. My husband of forty-seven years, the Love of my life, has transitioned to glory and is no longer on this earth with me. It took God and the friends He sent my way to walk me through the valley. It is beyond the shadow to the reality that God is by my side and leading me out of the valley. I stand today, knowing that I am more than a conqueror through Him that loves me (Romans 8:37).

Prayer

Father God, help me to walk through the valleys in my life. Help me to walk out of my painful and negative situations and walk into the newness of life in Christ Jesus, knowing Your Word tells me if any man be in Christ, he is a new creature. Old things have passed away and all things are new. Thank you, Father, for renewing me. Today is my new day. Amen (2 Cor. 5:17).

Pastor Geraldine Findley

CONTRIBUTORS

Alice Farrell, JD. LCSW, is an Evangelist with Church of God of Prophecy in Springfield, MA. She is a Sunday School teacher and Youth Director. Her interest is to build capacity through teaching, preaching and writing. President & CEO of Olive Branch Clinical and Consulting Services, LLC. She is an International Trainer, author and Clinical Consultant.

Alicia Morgan lives to encourage and empower the body of Christ. She attends Rehoboth Church of God in Bloomfield Connecticut and currently serves in various ministry capacities in and outside of her local church. She and her husband Bruce are blessed to parent two children, Nathan and Nia-Amora.

Andrea Boweya is a Registered Psychotherapist, Pre-Marriage and Marriage Relationship Coach. Author, Keynote and Inspirational Speaker. Andrea lives in Toronto, Canada.

Andrea C. Dunk is a long-standing member of Church of the Open Bible in May Pen, Jamaica. Her passion is to mentor young Christian women. She assists her father who is a retired Pastor in the areas of visitation and praying for the sick. She enjoys gardening, reading and writing.

Byron G.E. Peart D.Min. is a Bishop with the New Testament Church of God. He is the Pastor of Emanuel Temple of Prayer Church of God in West Hartford, Connecticut. He is also an Adjunct Professor at Hartford Seminary and Pentecostal Theological Seminary (PTS). Dr. Peart serves as Regional Coordinator for Calling and Ministry Studies Program as well as Reginal Coordinator of PTS Cohort Certificate Program. He is married to

Georgia Peart.

Charlton Daley is Pastor at Solid Rock Church of God in Manchester, Connecticut. He enjoys being a shepherd and loves teaching the Word of God. His wife, Janet, is also a Minister.

Clara Ruffin, along with her husband, is the co-Pastor at the Open Door Ministries in Hartford, Connecticut. Among her many talents, she has written several books. She also creates and publishes inspirational cards.

Coleene Shaw is a member of Rehoboth Church of God in Bloomfield, Connecticut. She sings in the choir and is active in other ministries.

Diane Crosley-Mayers and her husband Robert, attend Travis Air Force Base Gospel Church in California. Her passion is to teach and provide ministerial support. She enjoys reading and visiting with friends.

Donna Maxwell is an active member of Rehoboth Church of God in Bloomfield, Connecticut. She serves as the Superintendent of Sunday School and is actively involved in Youth and Discipleship, Bible study and Missions Ministries. Her passion is to be productive for God wherever He places her. She enjoys writing poetry and walking on the beach.

Dorothy Rowland is a member of Rehoboth Church of God in Bloomfield, Connecticut. She is a graduate of the MIP program and is a minister at her church. She volunteers with Missions, Evangelism, Soup Kitchen and Chaplaincy.

Elaine Beckford is an ordained minister at Rehoboth Church of God in Bloomfield, Connecticut. She is in charge of the Prayer Ministry and faithfully fulfils her calling.

G.A.T. Lives in Toronto, Canada

Geraldine Finley is the Pastor and Founder of Christian Community Outreach Church, in Hartford, Connecticut since 1988. She is the host of a weekly radio broadcast. She enjoys encouraging and enlightening people.

Hannah (Grace) Fevrier is a member of "New Church Without Walls" in Hernando, Florida. Her minister is Bishop Douglas Alexander. Hannah helps with Hospitality and Help ministries. She enjoys traveling, along with spending time with her grandchildren.

Irene Stewart is an 83-year-old "church mother." She has taught the Seniors in Sunday School for many years.

J.A.T. Lives in Richmond Hill, Canada.

Rev. John S. Murray is a minister who lives in Trenton, New Jersey. He is currently planting and building a church near Montego Bay, Jamaica.

Joy Wilson along with her husband Elder Anthony Wilson are active members of Rehoboth Church of God. She has been a Sunday School teacher for many years along with being involved in other activities in the church.

Kareen Jackson is a member of the Church of the Open Bible in May Pen, Clarendon, Jamaica.

Kathleen Beckford Davids, deceased 2019, lived in Queens, New York and was a member of Queens Church of the Firstborn, Inc. Her passion was for singing.

Kirk Burke is an ordained minister at Rehoboth Church of God. He is an engineer by profession and plays the keyboard for the church's worship service. He is a Bible teacher.

Laverne Ramsey is the wife of Bishop Johnathon Ramsey, Jr., Senior Pastor at Rehoboth Church of God in Bloomfield, Connecticut. She is an ordained minister and a teacher in the Hartford School System. She oversees the Women's Ministry at her church.

Lenore Kidd is Pastor Emeritus Dabar Bethlehem Cathedral (formerly Bethlehem Missionary Church) Queens Village, New York. Pastor Kidd is retired and presently resides with her husband Rev. Stanley Kidd in Clermont, Florida.

Lillian Turnipseed is an ordained minister. She is the First Lady of the Beacon Avenue Church of God in Providence, Rhode Island. Rev. Turnipseed is the Coordinator for the Southern New England Ministerial Internship Program. She is also involved in many ministries in the church.

Marva Tyndale M.Th. is the Founder/Director, Real Identity Discovery Ministries. Author, Preacher-Teacher, keynote speaker. Rev Tyndale lives in Toronto, Canada, www.realidteaching.org

Michaelia Daubon is the Assistant Pastor at Celestial Praise Church of God. She has a heart for people who have had adverse childhood experiences and trauma. She helps people in processing, healing and moving forward. Rev Daubon loves the creative and expressive arts, audiobooks and teaching.

Mildred Shaw is an ordained minister at Rehoboth Church of God in Bloomfield, Connecticut. She is very devoted to her church where she serves as the Director of Chaplaincy.

Monica Case Williams is a member of Tabernacle of

Praise International Church in McDonough, Georgia. She is a member of the Prayer Intercessor Team as well as the Events Planning Team. Her interest is as a Good News Club Worker and Minister/Pray by Phone. Monica was also very instrumental in the publication of this Devotional.

Nessa Oram-Edwards attends Living Water Fellowship, Poinciana, Florida. She is secretary to Agape Missions International, Inc. She is the leader of small group and Women for Christ Prayer Ministry.

Nora M. Brown is a retired schoolteacher, having taught in the public school for nearly 40 years. She is a communicant at St. Monica Episcopal Church in Hartford, Connecticut. She is a very active member of various ministries in the church. She is married to a stalwart in the community, Dermoth Brown.

Paulette Joseph is an active member of Rehoboth Church of God in Bloomfield, Connecticut. She is involved in several ministries within the church, along with being a Sunday School teacher and singing in the choir.

Pauline Washington is a member of Sanctuary of Faith and Glory in Windsor, Connecticut. She teaches the Bible and enjoys studying God's Word

Pearl Huggins is an ordained minister at Rehoboth Church of God. She serves on the Pastor's Council and is a Sunday School teacher. Most notably, she is the Director of the Senior Ministry. Rev Huggins does an excellent job working with the Seniors and is held in high regards by all of them.

Percival Young is a Trustee at First Baptist Church in West Hartford, Connecticut. He is very active in the church. He is married to Lorna Young.

Phenice McLean is a Minister at Rehoboth Church of God in Bloomfield, Connecticut and serves on the Pastor's Council. She is the Director of Stewardship at her church. She is a Sunday School teacher as well as a Bible Study teacher. She loves the Lord and serves her church faithfully.

Rosalind Smallhorne is the church Administrator at Rehoboth Church of God in Bloomfield, Connecticut. Active in every aspect of the church. She also works with the State of Connecticut.

Sandra Rhone is the Senior Pastor at Ever-lasting Hope Ministries in Windsor, Connecticut. Her ministries include, Pastoral, Chaplaincy and Mothers United in Prayer. Her interest includes health and nutrition.

Sheila Hoyte is a retired secondary school Vice Principal. She and her husband live in Metro Toronto, enjoying their grandchildren. Highest ambition is seeking to be "found in Him, not having my own righteousness."

Sherill Thomas is an Ordained Minister and an affiliate of Grace Christian Fellowship in Florida. Her ministerial gifts include counseling, teaching and writing. Her passion is to help others live their best lives which she believes can only be found in doing the will of God.

Sonia Brown is a determined believer in the Word of God. She has been walking with the Lord since 1993. Presently worshiping at Bramalea Christian Fellowship, Brampton, Ontario, Canada. Sonia loves the Ministry of Prayer with a passion for missions.

Stephanie Lightfoot is retired from the Travelers Insurance Company. She is Senior Warden and Lay

Minister at St Monica's Episcopal Church in Hartford, Connecticut.

Rev. Stonewall Hunter, Jr. is the Senior Pastor at True Vine Missionary Baptist Church in Bastrop, Louisiana. He loves to travel with his wife and family and enjoys sharing his faith.

Terry Joseph is an ordained minister at Rehoboth Church of God in Bloomfield, Connecticut. She serves on the Church Council and teaches Bible Studies.

Tracy Russel-Johnson is the Rector at St Monica's Episcopal Church in Hartford, Connecticut. Her ministries include: Your Place Hartford, Ruth Smalls Food Pantry and St Monica's Feeding Program. Her interest includes Social Justice and Community Advocacy.

Ursula Brown is a member of Pilgrim Way Baptist Church in Windsor, CT. She is President of the Missionary Board. She is a nurse by profession and enjoys working out.

Yvonne Mitto is an ordained minister at Crossroads Community Cathedral. Executive Director Compass- New England & Certified Coach. Trainer and speaker with the John Maxwell Team. Rev Mitto works with Pastors and leaders to equip people in the area of biblical financial stewardship and help foster a culture of financial discipleship and generosity in their churches and faith-based organizations.

ABOUT THE AUTHOR

Beverly Coker is an ordained minister at Rehoboth Church of God in Bloomfield, Connecticut. She is involved in several ministries within the church and is also very active in the community. She has written and published much about various aspects of the West Indian community. Coker holds a master's degree in social work and a doctorate in Education from the University of Connecticut (UCONN). She is a retired school administrator, a preacher, teacher, and a motivational speaker.

Coker is the wife of Tom Coker to whom she has been married for 40 years. They have two adult children. She is also a grandmother.

She can be reached at becoker@hotmail.com

Made in the USA
Monee, IL
13 January 2020

20217674R00184